# AN IRISH NAVVY

## The Diary of an Exile

by

### DONALL Mac AMHLAIGH

Translated from the Irish by
VALENTIN IREMONGER

**Routledge and Kegan Paul**
LONDON AND HENLEY

First published in England 1964
Published as a Routledge paperback 1966
by Routledge and Kegan Paul Limited
39 Store Street
London WC1E 7DD and
Broadway House, Newtown Road
Henley-on-Thames, Oxon. RG9 1EN
Reprinted 1970, 1971 and 1976
Printed in Great Britain by
Lowe & Brydone Printers Limited
Thetford, Norfolk

ISBN 0 7100 2854 7

Translated from the Irish
DIALANN DEORAÍ
© An Clóchomhar Tta, Dublin

# Contents

# Preface

---

Donall Mac Amhlaigh was born a short distance outside
Galway in 1926. His schooling followed a normal pattern in
Ireland in the thirties and forties—elementary school followed
by a period of secondary education. At the age of fifteen, he had
to leave school and he worked for three years in a woollen mill
in Kilkenny where his family had gone to live a year or so
beforehand. Galway, however, had cast its spell on him and he
found that he could not avoid going back to that lovely city in
the west of Ireland that, even in its contemporary development,
manages to epitomise so much of what makes up the Irish
character and sense of history. There he worked on farms,
interspersed with periods as a waiter in various hotels, before
he joined the First Batallion of the Irish Army. This is an Irish-
speaking unit and in it, he spent what he still regards as the
most enjoyable three years of his life. And who, particularly
loving Irish as Mr. Mac Amhlaigh does, wouldn't look back
nostalgically to three years in Galway where the busy com-
mercial streets and the beautiful surrounding countryside echo
to the music of a vigorous and expressive tongue?

When Mr. Mac Amhlaigh left the Army in 1951, Ireland
was still in a stage of underdevelopment and there was fairly
heavy unemployment. He followed the pattern of the times,
emigrated to England and joined those of his countrymen
without whose help the British Health Service and the
building, light engineering and service industries would have
ground to a standstill. This book is an account of his first

six years in a highly industrialised society for the impact of which he was unprepared but the shock of which, with the resilience of his race, he absorbed. As I write he still works, from choice, on a constructional site near Northampton, where with his wife and two children, he lives contentedly, wielding his pick and shovel by day and his gifted pen by night.

It will be seen that Mr. Mac Amhlaigh, in his first years in exile, speaks with some bitterness of the necessity that made him leave Ireland to earn a living. Understandably enough, he is inclined to blame the authorities but one must look further than that to account for the slowness of development in Ireland during the first thirty years of the State's existence  Leaving aside the chequered history of Ireland up to 1800, I draw a veil over economic affairs in Ireland from the Act of Union with Britain until 1922. Suffice it to note that, after a war of independence from 1916 to 1921 which took its economic toll, a bitter Civil War ensued; the economic effects of both were felt throughout the twenties. In the thirties, the State was in the throes of economic war with Britain which was only resolved in 1938 by which time the guns of the Second World War were being massed and, a year later, used. It was not, therefore, until 1945 that the authorities were able to think in terms of expansion rather than simple survival. From then on, the picture started changing. Slowly and laboriously, the young State built the 'infra-structure' without which economic development cannot take place—housing, hospitals, health services, social welfare services, power, roads, transport, the distributive industry. And then, with the publication of the First Programme for Economic Expansion in 1958, what has come to be called the Irish Economic Miracle was on its way. The Second Programme, which sets desired objectives to be achieved by 1970, has so far maintained the impetus of the years 1958–63 and the outlook for the future is, with hard work by all concerned, bright. Mr. Mac Amhlaigh would, I think, agree that conditions in Ireland have changed enormously since the time he found it necessary to leave his homeland.

The present book, entitled in Irish *Dialann Deorai* (The Diary of an Exile) was one of the most notable and successful books to appear in the Irish language in recent years. It is a remarkable piece of documentary writing, but it bears all the marks of the creative artist in its attention to detail, its shrewd observation both of person and place and, not least, in its author's ability to tell a story well. In the original, a further characteristic was evident in the author's awareness of, and interest in, the texture and rhythm of the language in which he wrote.

Mr. Mac Amhlaigh was not born with Irish yet he handles the language with all the confidence of one who has profited by many hours spent in the company of those who had it from the cradle. His understanding of the nature of the language and of its idiom, coupled with a feeling for the individual word and phrase, shows that he has given much thought to the problems confronting him as a writer. If the Irish which he uses is not always that of the native speaker, this is the conscious result of his desire to write the Irish that is widely spoken today in its inevitable development from the older 'pure' language of the Gaeltacht. This alone gives his book a particular importance in the current renaissance that is taking place in Irish literature.

Apart from that, however, his book is an honest account of how the average Irish labourer works, lives in, and makes his contribution to, the development of the country that has given him a good wage for the sweat of his brow.

VALENTIN IREMONGER

*Stockholm,*
*August, 1964.*

# 1

# Ward Orderly

The mother saw the ad. in the paper: 'Stokers wanted. Live in. Apply Matron, Harborough Rd. Hospital, Northampton.'

'You could give it a chance,' she said, 'for surely God put it in your way.'

I had been idle the three months since I had left the Army and, as I had to go across anyway, it was as well for me to try this rather than go on spec and wander around looking for lodgings after I had landed. I wrote my letter and off it went and, in God's good time, an answer came in a couple of days. The mother and myself watched every post, our hearts in our mouths all the time hoping for good news. As soon as the answer came, however, both of us got very melancholy, thinking how I'd be leaving home and going foreign. The mother and I had always been very close and, although we both knew that sooner or later I'd have to be off with myself, we were both very much affected at the prospect. My mother called in from the street one of the children playing around there and sent her off to the shop for a sweet cake so that we'd have a celebration in honour of the occasion. As she took up the pot to make the tea, I could see that her eyes were brimming with tears.

I started off on the business straight away. There were enough formalities to be gone through—not like today—and I was afraid that, if I spent too much time getting myself ready, I'd lose the job. I had to get a passport photo of myself taken and then go and fill up forms at the police station so that I could get an identity card. When that had all been done and when I had written over to the matron, I settled back to wait on the great day. I knew that I'd have to wait about a fortnight.

I felt pretty fed up most of the time then. I had dug the garden but it was a bit too early to sow anything; so that, after signing on at the 'Labour' in the morning, damn the thing I had to do except knock around wherever I pleased. And I can tell you there were plenty of places worth visiting at that time of the year over the rich lands of the County Kilkenny with the spring coming up. For nearly ten years we had been living in Kilkenny after leaving Galway (barring three years I spent in the First Battalion in Renmore just outside Galway City); it was a pity, in a way, that I only got to like the place just as I was about to leave it.

The day after I got news from the hospital, I whistled up the dog and struck out towards Callan with Mick Hogan. It was a fine evening and Mick's little dog and our own Toppy were more than happy as they frolicked around in front of us. There wasn't a scree, a hole or a ditch that they didn't examine and they'd let a yelp out of them from time to time as they smelt the trail of a rabbit or a rat. As we left the city behind us, majestic Slievenamon towered regally in front of us while, away to the south, Mount Leinster and the Blackstairs range lay under a beautiful purple haze. All around us, the rough voices of the crows could be heard raucously chattering to each other with, occasionally, the sweet music of the blackbird as it welcomed such a good day.

The mild healthy country air was like a tonic to my friend and the evening passed quickly as he told me about the various dangers he had faced while he had been a soldier in the *Connaughts*.* Sadly I parted from Old Mick that evening, thinking that maybe I'd never see him again now that I was off to England.

Quickly enough the days went by and, as the time for leaving drew nearer, I could feel the cold talons of despair twining and

* The Connaught Rangers who mutinied in India in 1920 in protest against the Black and Tan atrocities in Ireland.

untwining inside me. I knew that I'd miss the small ordinary things that I had been used to for so long: the company and the kind chat with the lads down at the corner every night; the good-fellowship and the gaiety of the poor people in the 'four-pennies' at the pictures on pay-night; and the excellence of the pints in Larry's pub after closing time. I knew I'd be lonesome too for the sprees and the fun we used to have in our own house from time to time. My sister and two of my brothers were home at that time; my father and another brother were in the Army—one in Cork, the other in Dublin. A garrulous family we were always—'all wit and no wisdom', as the old lady used to say—and whatever there was to eat on the table, you can be sure that it was flavoured with memorable conversation.

Now above all, I felt like staying at home for ever if I could only have found anything to do: but I hadn't the luck. I was getting twenty-two and six from the Labour Exchange and that wasn't enough to keep anybody. As it was now near enough to my departure time, I said to myself that, before leaving, I'd walk around all those places that were dearest to me. I was very disappointed that I hadn't the money to visit Galway and Renmore and maybe West Connemara too where some of the friends I liked best lived; but I had hardly the price of the odd pint, let alone the bus fare to where my people came from.

*Monday, 12.3.1951.* This morning I signed on for the last time and then carried a hundredweight of coal home for my mother. I have everything done for her now, the garden planted and cleaned and the old house spruced up a bit on the outside. I'll be able to help her a bit more than that from now on when I'll have the few pence to send to her from England.

I spent the day putting some kind of order into the old box that I keep my papers in and then I went around saying good-bye to the neighbours. Peter's wife was very sorry at my going, the creature. She was kindness itself always and, as for the other people in the district, it would be hard to surpass them. I'd have liked nothing better than to have been able to visit my relatives and old friends back in Galway but, alas! I've only enough to get me across the water with a bit to spare.

The old lady kept her courage up wonderfully until the time

came for me to set off. The tears came then. I didn't delay too long bidding her good-bye. I hugged her once, grabbed my bag and off with me. Indeed, you'd think that even the cat knew I was going for she followed me out mewing piteously.

I stood at the head of the boreen to look back at the house, and there I saw my mother with her left hand up to her mouth as was her habit whenever she was worried about something.

Who did I meet then, as I was crossing the bridge, but Sonny Campbell. Sonny spent a long time in the British Navy and anyone would think that he gets money from the British Government for sending people over from Ireland to join up. He's always running down this country, saying that it's ridiculous for people to stay here seeing the good wages to be had beyond. Some of the lads have a bit of devilment with him, rising him and quizzing him about life over there; but I've noticed that Sonny himself shows no sign of moving across.

He paused when he saw the bag that I was carrying. 'Are you crossing over?' he enquired, with some satisfaction you might think.

'I am, brother,' I said.

'Good man,' he replied rubbing his hands together, 'it won't be long till there's nobody left here at all. They're all going. What is there for them here? You'll never regret it. It won't be long till I'll be crossing myself. Well, good luck to you.'

He shook hands with me and took himself off, as pleased as if I had pressed a half-sovereign into his fist.

Old Johnny Brennan, the Fenian,* was waiting for me outside Smyth's and we went in for a last drink before my departure. The poor man is of a great age—he must be going ninety and, God knows, I mightn't see him again. When the man of the house himself heard where I was off to, nothing would do him but to stand us another drink. It was generous of him, to tell you the truth, for it was seldom enough we went into his pub. The world and its mother knows that I was very upset at having to leave the old Fenian and, indeed, he felt the same about the whole affair.

As I went on to the platform to get on the train, my old dog

* A member of the Fenian Brotherhood who were responsible for the Rising of 1865 against British rule in Ireland.

Toppy was at my heels, however the devil he managed to follow me without my being aware of him. He looked so lonely sitting there on the platform that a lump came into my throat as the train pulled out.

I kept my nose to the window until Three Castles, Dunmore and Ballyfoyle were out of sight. I sat back then and wasn't interested in anything else.

There was a good crowd on the boat with me. The *Princess Maud* we were on and my courage came back to me quickly enough once I found myself amongst them. Before I had been two minutes aboard, who did I meet but the big fellow from Tooreen who had come into Renmore last year to enlist; and a girl from the same place with him. They were off to London and there was another girl from round about Oughterard with them also. We got together straight away and I didn't feel at all lonely while I was with them. The Irish of the girl from Oughterard wasn't as good as the Irish the other two spoke but there was nothing wrong with her apart from that. I met many people from those parts that hadn't any Irish at all.

We had only time to have a drop of tea when the boat started moving and before we knew where we were, we were edging away from the quay. I got well to the back of the boat to have a good gander at Ireland and the bright lights north there of Dun Laoire; and, suddenly, I felt lonely all over again. I started thinking about the old house with the pots of tea that we'd drink before going to bed and my heart felt like a solid black mass inside my breast.

I didn't leave the place until the last light had sunk out of sight. Only then did I go looking for the other three.

I stood on John Bull's territory for the first time in my life on Tuesday morning when I got off the Irish Mail at Rugby. I don't count Holyhead for that's really Welsh and there was as much Welsh spoken there as there was Irish on a fair day in Derrynea. I lost my friends in the customs hall and I never saw them again. And what a to-do there was about our bags! You'd think that we were carrying priceless jewels instead of the few old rags we had. There was one man who shoved on to the counter an old battered case that was tied with a bit of rope to keep it shut.

'What have you got here?' said the customs officer.

'Yerra, nothing at all,' said my lad with a grin.

'Open it up, all the same,' said your man.

'Sure, it's hardly worth my while,' said the lad.

'Look here, you're only wasting both our time. I can't let you through until you open up that bag.'

'Fair enough,' said my lad and drew out of his pocket a bloody big knife with which he cut the rope around the case. The lid jumped up just like a Jack-in-the-Box and out leapt an old pair of Wellington boots that had been twisted up inside it. Devil the thing else was in the case—not even a change of socks. A melancholy wintry little smile crossed the face of the customs officer as he motioned to your man to get along with himself.

I slept most of the way from there to Rugby and, when I left the train, I had a two-hour delay before I caught the train to Northampton. My heart sank altogether then as I stood and looked around at the dirty ugly station. Everything looked so foreign to me there. Round about six o'clock hundreds started pouring into the station, pallid pasty faces with identical lunch boxes slung from their shoulders. They were all getting the train to work and their likes were getting off the train at the same time coming to work in Rugby, I suppose. God save us, I murmured to myself as I thought that nobody in Ireland would be even thinking of getting out of their beds for another couple of hours yet!

I reached Northampton by eight o'clock on a slow train that took three-quarters of an hour to do that short journey. On all sides, there was nothing to be seen but farming land and cattle; and I felt my isolation more and more as I saw that I was right in the heart of England where I was unlikely to meet a single Irishman. The black chimney stacks of London would have been preferable just then as I knew that I'd have met some of my own people there whatever else.

As I got off the train at Northampton, I enquired about the hospital and a man said that he was going in that direction on the bus and that I might as well go with him. I didn't know from God what he was saying most of the time but I gathered that he was a Catholic married to a Roscommon woman and

6

that she had converted him. When I got off the bus, I had only another quarter-mile to go. I slung my bag up on my shoulder and started off without any more delay.

Some oul' wan took me in hand when I got to the hospital door and got me a bit of breakfast. There was a foreign crowd in the canteen when I got there and I was told that they were D.P.'s—Ukrainians and Poles and suchlike—that had been driven from their homes during the war. When I had eaten my meal—and, God knows, it wasn't hard to dispose of a drop of tea and a bit of bread and jam—I was brought in to the matron so that she could tell me the conditions under which I would work and all that sort of thing. I was supposed to be taking up a job as a boilerman; but after a few minutes' conversation, she asked me would I not prefer to be an orderly instead. I said that I didn't mind one way or the other but that I thought I'd be a better hand with the old shovel; but she wheedled me so much into taking the other job that in the end I agreed.

Then I went to bed to rid myself of the weariness of the journey. Soundly indeed I slept and didn't waken until five o'clock. After shaving and washing, I made my way down to supper and, God knows, I felt shy enough going down among all the nurses in the canteen. It wasn't the same room that I had been in during the morning for it seems that the nurses and the orderlies have a canteen to themselves apart from the ward-maids and the boilermen. Some devilish stuff called spam was for supper accompanied by roast potatoes; but I was so hungry at this stage that I left not a single thing on my plate.

I mosied off down town then to see what kind of a place it was and I had a couple of pints of ale in some pub. I didn't care very much for this drink: it didn't stand up very well in comparison with a pint of porter. The pubs were nice and clean and the people pleasant enough but somehow or other I didn't take to them. There were games going on all the time in the pub— darts, skittles and suchlike with a jukebox screeching away all the time. I couldn't help comparing it with Larry's pub back home—the good wise chat and the manliness that I shared with those drinking there. The women are as plentiful in the pubs here as there are fleas on a goat and no man can be at ease wherever they are.

I spent some time talking to the man that was in the room with me. Bert was his name. He was a nice decent man, it seemed, and I got on quite well with him. He was from Cambridge and maybe that's why I understood him so well.

I started the next morning in Ward 1. I had to wear a white coat over my own clothes and I felt a bit of a fool in that rig-out. This was a children's ward and I found them all mannerly enough, the poor things. There was a nice nurse with me there—a Lithuanian—but her English was good. I don't know that I'll like this place at all but I doubt it. It's the devil and all to have to be working with women.

I was given the lead polisher (as Paddy Ryan used to call it back in Renmore) to work and, in no time at all, I had a fine sheen on the floor. The women showed some surprise at my being so good. Little they thought that I spent many a day with the same yoke when I was C.B. in the Army. It's mostly Irish girls that are here between nurses and others but they weren't very Gaelic—the bunch I saw anyhow. God be with the wonderful girls back there in Connemara! It didn't take very long to get to know them at a dance or a hooley; but so far as this gang of Irish is concerned, I feel more of a foreigner with them than I do with the foreigners themselves.

I wrote a short letter home to the old lady and then I went out with Tommy Power from County Waterford, a young lad that's working here. We went down to the Royal Oak (every pub here had its own special name) and had a couple of pints. A bottle of Guinness costs one and twopence here (compared with sevenpence at home) and it has a bitter enough flavour. You never hear tell of a pint of porter here but the Irish drink pints of stout and mild—a sweetish mixture that they think is something like the pint of porter.

The air is very healthy in these parts.

There's no doubt about it but the nurse that works with me is a lovely woman. I passed a good part of the day talking to her, discoursing about this language and that and I thought that a lot of the words in her own tongue were similar enough to words that we have in Irish.

I'm afraid, from what I have seen so far, in this place, that the Irish girls don't come within an ass's roar of the 'foreigners' so far as deportment, manners and that sort of thing is concerned. They have an ugly fashion of screeching with laughter in the canteen and they have the most revolting English idioms at the tips of their tongues—such as 'you've had it, mate', and 'crikey'. There's something demeaning about the Irish person that imitates the English or other people. I don't think that, even if I was here until Doomsday, I'd ever acquire any of the unpleasant idioms that they use around the place.

I went down for the Rosary and then walked slowly home afterwards. Damn this place, there's nothing in it. Bad and all as it might be, there's more in Kilkenny!

I was really fed up with myself today for a while as I thought about the times we had in the Army back in Renmore. All right—you might have good enough pay over here but by the time my keep was deducted there was only about four quid left for myself. And a wise little head from Waterford was telling me that I'd only get two days pay this week because they usually keep you a week in arrears until you're leaving.

I went down to the National Insurance Office this afternoon to get a ration book, an identity card and an insurance card. In this country everybody has to have these papers and I'd say it would go hard with you to put a foot in front of you without notifying the authorities. They were wonderfully pleasant in the office, unlike their kind back home in Ireland and I was finished with the business without too much delay. I then walked around the town for a while and I was surprised at the size of the people there. I had always thought that the English were small people but it seems that in these parts they are very tall and you'd never think from them that they hadn't had enough to eat for years.

Another thing that you couldn't help noticing was how well-dressed they were compared with the people back home. I didn't see a single person with threadbare clothes or worn-out footwear. Clothes and much else are dearer here than in Ireland and I'm thinking that I'd be well advised to go home to Ireland once a year and fit myself out.

I got a great wish for a handful of sweets but I couldn't buy them as I hadn't any coupons. I went into one of the big stores and had a drop of tea. I thought for a long time about my old comrades in the Army—Ward, Colum the Champion and Michael Saile's son—the lot of them. They're all over here now if one only knew where to look for them.

Tomorrow is St. Patrick's Day and there's great talk among the Irish about the Feast.

*Feast of St. Patrick of the Gael.* A box of shamrock arrived from home this morning. I was free for the first part of the day and I went out to Mass. I couldn't believe that there were so many people from Ireland in the city. Every fourth person that I met had the shamrock up and the church was full to overflowing. After Mass, they hung around outside the church just as they do at home and I have to say that I never saw such fine strong men and such lovely girls for a long time. I was pleased and proud to see them like that for those up where I work are pretty poor types.

I wandered off down the city by myself and dropped into a pub where the Irish gathered. To tell you the truth I wouldn't have been able to go in for a drink but for the fact that Bert, my room-mate, gave me a pound that morning. He asked me if I was going out for a few drinks in honour of the Saint. I said I wasn't. He then tried to find out the reason for this as he found it incredible that an Irishman wouldn't have a drink on St. Patrick's Day. He sensed soon enough what the trouble was and he said nothing more but pressed a paper pound into my hand. There was one generous Englishman for you although as a race they're not noted for liberality.

The *Admiral Rodney* was the name of the pub I dropped into and it was full to the doorways with fine Irish boys, all of them knocking back their pints. I made my way in and got a drink for myself, keeping an eye out the whole time in case I'd see a man from Connemara. There weren't any there, however; it seemed that most of the men were from the County Mayo. These lads had none of the foreign airs that the women up at the hospital had and, but for their being dressed so well, you'd have thought that you were back in a pub in the West of Ireland on a fair-day.

They have the habit here—the Irish as well as everybody

else—of moving from pub to pub instead of staying in the one place as we do at home. When the fun was at its highest in the *Rodney*, the boys started moving off. At first, I thought they were going off home for their dinner but when I asked one of the men he said no, they were going down to the *Bull*. The crowd down there would come up to the *Rodney* and so on. I thought to myself that I had better get down to the *Bull* to see what was going on there that was different from here so I followed the crowd out.

The lads here are very friendly and, unless you were careful, you'd be in the company in no time and they'd be buying drinks for you. I wasn't in any position to be joining company like that for I had only the pound Bert had given me and I wanted to keep something out of it for later in the evening.

One of the men down at the *Bull* had an accordion and was knocking great music out of it. There was hardly a jig or a hornpipe that he didn't play and I could feel the heart rising inside me. I'd have given anything to have been able to stay until closing time but I had to go on duty at one o'clock and I was late for the dinner already.

It's a long spell from one until eight but, somehow, I didn't notice it passing. Devil the much I had to do there in the children's section bar keeping the place clean and going round with the meals. But they tell me that I'll be changing over on Monday to a section where I'll have more to do.

I moved off down town after supper and I found it hard enough to get away without that young devil Nicholas knowing about it. I had a drink or two (I couldn't buy more) and I saw a lot of the boys blind drunk by this time. I went to the dance then and, although I had never been there before, I had no difficulty in finding the place, there were so many making their way there. The band wasn't all that good and there were only one or two Irish dances the whole night.

A couple of fights started but those taking part were thrown out as soon as they got rough. There's a big strong priest from County Cork there, Father James Galvin, and he's six and a half feet tall if he's an inch. He's in charge of the Irish Club and, as the dance was being run by the club, he was responsible for keeping the peace at it. He and another sturdy man went in amongst those who were fighting and threw them out of the door just as you'd throw out rubbish that you had no use for. That was the end of the ructions.

There was a small group of women inside also and most of them came from the place where I was working. I can't say that I enjoyed that night all that much. God be with this night last year and the great Irish spree we had in Curran's in Galway—Ward, Kerry, Michael Jim and myself. They were men whose company was worth while.

Sunday morning I had to get up very early as I had to get first Mass since I had to be on duty until one o'clock. That's the worst of this place—that you have to work different shifts all the time. I was free from one until five and I spent the afternoon writing a few letters home.

There are so many languages being spoken here that it's worse than the Tower of Babel. You can hear Italian, Ukrainian, German and Lithuanian on all sides but, alas! not a word of Irish. I must teach a few words to that wild devil, Nicholas; it's not so long since he left school so it shouldn't be too hard to get him speaking it again. He wouldn't be here at all but for the fact that his sister is a nurse in the hospital and she brought him over from Ireland so that he wouldn't break his mother's heart altogether. They have a farm at home but since the father died, there was no controlling Nicholas. He is to be sent out to New York as soon as possible; and it's a damn pity he's not going tomorrow.

He's a sturdy boy and, although he's not yet eighteen years old, he's as strong as a bull. He has me pestered because all the men working here are either D.P.'s or Englishmen and Nick dislikes the whole lot of them. He regards himself as a first-rate loyal Irishman and he thinks that the best way he can show his loyalty is by perpetually fighting with the English and the foreigners. His sister came over this morning to ask me to look after him as she thought I might help to improve him. It's more likely that he'll find himself on his backside on the floor if he doesn't leave me a bit of peace!

But to go back to the question of languages, the foreign people here have an amazing grasp of them. Apart from the

Italians, there isn't a national group that isn't able to speak about four languages. For instance, the Ukrainians are able to speak German, Polish and a little Lithuanian; the Germans and the Poles are the same. There are about ten Italians here and they only speak their own tongue but probably because they never had to leave their own country like the others. Except for one woman, they're all from Naples and they're marvellous musicians. They live for singing and they have a life and vigour in them that nobody else has.

The woman here from the north of Italy has no regard at all for the other Italians that are here and she says that they are dirty and lazy at home. That can't be said about them here, however, and they are a gay and lively crowd. It is as maids they work here since they have so little English. Some of the other foreigners work as hospital orderlies, or as assistant nurses; the English and the Irish have the best jobs. For example, the matron is English of Irish extraction; the deputy matron and half the sisters are Irish.

I still had the price of the dance in the Irish Club (eighteenpence) left over from yesterday so I went down about an hour before the end. There was a fine gathering of girls there; and who should I meet but my old friend, Stephen O'Toole, (Steve Darby) from Spiddal. We spent at least a half an hour talking about Spiddal and the great *ceilis* that went on there in our day. Two lads were needling one another in the hall all the night and, when the dance was over, they asked the priest to give them the boxing gloves and to act as referee for them. When all the women were gone, the doors were locked and we gathered around to see the fight. They spent half an hour skipping around one another and falling and holding without either of them damaging the other until the priest had to send them packing off home in the end.

'Fighters,' he said in disgust, 'sure you'd beat them with your cap.'

But they tell me that there's many a good hard fight takes place there under the priest's auspices. Father Galvin believes that whatever enmity may arise between a couple of men, it's better settled there in the Club rather than have them fighting it out in the street and giving bad example to the pagans.

Stephen walked home a bit of the way with me and we talked for a good while before we finally parted. He was amazed to find me working in the hospital and he advised me to get out of it as I'd get twice as much pay working with him on the navvying. Maybe I'll do it, too!

I started to try to teach Nick some Irish. Though he'd like to know it, however, the devil hasn't enough patience to learn anything. We made up a plan to pull the wool over the eyes of the foreigners so as to pretend that we always spoke Irish among ourselves. Nick knew a good deal of songs from school and what we arranged to do whenever anybody would be listening to us, was that I would say conversationally a line of poetry: 'What will we do without timber?' Nick would then answer with the next line: 'The last of the forest is down'; I would follow with the next line and so on. We planned to laugh now and again and to appear to be angry from time to time. We got a chance to do it this afternoon when there were some Poles and Ukrainians standing around the back door enjoying the first bit of sun I've seen since I came here. Nick and I came to the door pretending that we were delighted to see the sun shining at last. I looked up at the sun and then as if I was commenting on the weather, I remarked: 'What will we do without timber?'

'Oh! be gor, the last of the forest is down,' said the lad.

I stretched myself lazily and said:

'Kilcash and its house are forgotten.'

'And its bell will be heard no more,' said Nick. I let on that I was feeling a bit down and I made a face.

'And what the divil about that place where the oul' wan lived?' I said.

Nick gave me a kick on the ankle.

'Stick to your —— lines,' he said venomously. I had put him off his stroke with my improvisation and he couldn't think of what came after the idea in that line. I rescued him then, however, with:

'The duck or the goose won't be heard there.'

'Or the eagle above the bay,' he replied.

The foreigners were all ears by now and I could see that they were amazed at all this Irish. They started looking at us with a new respect, even that Ukrainian Pizzarenko whom Nick was always annoying and challenging. We were well away, I'm telling you, but for Nick's sister arriving at that very moment and hearing what we were at.

'Well, there's a good man,' she said to me, 'teaching Nicky Irish and when he was at home he'd learn nothing.'

All the foreigners burst out laughing and Nick almost jumped up a mile in the air in a fit of rage. He threw a malevolent glance at Pizzarenko and started leaping around with his two fists up and shouting: 'All right, Pizzy, put them up. Come on and fight like a man. I'll teach you to laugh at the Irish.'

But your man Pizzy sloped off to his own room breaking his heart laughing.

Nick is in a blinding rage ever since· and it's not safe to talk to him, never mind anything else.

On Tuesday morning I started work in Ward 4 and there's a great difference between it and the first place. They are all adults in this ward—men with skin diseases (dermatitis and such like). I was anything but idle between sweeping out the floors, going around with meals and drinks and learning to put ointment on the limbs and bodies of the patients. There's a very nice girl working on the same shift as myself and I'm amazed that I didn't see her until today for the hospital isn't all that big. She's from Sligo and she's engaged to a Lithuanian from that camp up at Boughton. Pretty is hardly the word for her with her curly black hair, her lovely freckled brow and her two black eyes dancing with gaiety in her head. She talked about everything to me and, any time she could, she asked me into the kitchen for a drop of tea.

The doctor goes his round once a day and he's a real gentleman. They say that he's the best man on these illnesses in the whole country. Dr. Coles is his name. I can't get over how nice the doctors and others like them are in this country—quite different from home. Of all that are here, there's only one that's anyway arrogant and she's an Irishwoman.

This afternoon I had to go off and strip two of the patients and put this stuff they call Ingram's Ointment on them. I thoroughly disliked the whole business at first but then I began to pity the poor creatures and, after that, it didn't cost me a thought. They're all very kind and gentle and always very grateful for anything you do for them. I was finished at three o'clock.

A letter and a paper came from home. My mother is pleased that I'm working here as she thinks that I'd be far worse off out in lodgings. Maybe she's right, indeed, but the big money is tempting me away all the time.

On Wednesday, I finished at nine o'clock and I had to be back again at one. A strange thing happened to me then as I was going down Harborough Road to pay a visit to the church. I was passing a certain house when I noticed the name that was over the door—Earlsmere. Suddenly, I felt that I had been here some other time in my life standing outside the self-same house. It was as if I was waiting for someone and for a moment I expected to meet that person. It's not the first time that this has happened to me.

I didn't feel the evening passing as I was interested in the work. Some of the old men in the ward are from the small towns in these parts and their dialects are interesting enough. There's one Scotsman here, Mr. Gardiner, and he's in a terrible state—his whole skin peeling away in large dry flakes. He has a huge appetite and you have to keep watching him the whole time as he is not supposed to eat too much. I went to put a new bandage and some ointment on him and it was clear to me that the poor man didn't care what you did to him. He was perpetually shaking with the cold, and they tell me that it's the loss of the skin that's the cause of this. He was a train driver before he was laid low and isn't it sad to think that he's lying there now without understanding or perception or any of the things that he had to have to hold down such a job?

Visiting hours were from two until four o'clock and I was surprised to see how many people came to see their relatives. Mr. Gardiner's wife was the first in and she stayed until the very last minute. Twelve miles she has to travel to get here but they say that she never allows a day go by without coming in. Visitors are allowed three times a week, Wednesday, Saturday and Sunday, and on other days they are allowed to come to see the patients from a quarter to seven until a quarter to eight in the evenings.

I went down to the Rosary in the evening and met Steve Darby. He told me that Ward had got two months for assaulting a soldier down in Kidderminster.

Two pounds fourteen I drew on Thursday—three days' pay, God save the mark! I sent a pound of that home to the old lady. I went across to Kingsthorpe and bought myself a tin whistle and then spent the afternoon trying to get some semblance of music out of it. I managed 'Wrap the Green Flag Round Me, Boys' well enough but if I blew the thing for ever I couldn't get anything more complex out of it. Festie Conlon from Ballin-taggart was a great man at it but I'm afraid that I mustn't have any talent despite my love of music.

A new man came to work with us on a part-time basis. His name is Ray and he is studying at the university at Oxford. He's working here during the Easter vacation because although he's at Oxford his people aren't all that well off, and if he wants a bit of spare cash, he has to earn it himself. I had a very interesting conversation with him and he told me that I spoke 'remarkably good English'. He thought the Irish had betrayed themselves unconscionably when they forsook their own language. When I said that we got a good deal of help from his own people in forsaking the Irish language, he laughed at me.

'Oh, come, come,' he said, 'you're not going to tell me that we coerced you into dropping the Gaelic. We discouraged it, perhaps, but coercion—no!'

He got a good one over on Anita, the Italian maid working in our ward. We were both talking about languages and various other things as we were having a cup of coffee and Anita wanted to get us out of the kitchen so that she could clean it. She warned us a couple of times and when we paid no attention to her, she started cleaning all around us: and she was pretty annoyed, I can tell you. She let flow a stream of Italian at us to begin with and then she roared in English. 'All Irish dirty; all English lazy.'

'All Italians dirty *and* lazy,' Ray spat.

She grabbed her bucket of water and the floorcloth and I wouldn't think that it was a blessing she left with us as she swept out of the kitchen.

Worked until half past five on Good Friday. This is the shift we like best here; you're ready nice and early and there's plenty of time to go wherever you please. The girls who work here as wardmaids or assistant nurses only get between two pounds ten and three pounds depending on their age. The domestics, however, get about a pound more for some reason that I can't fathom since the assistant nurses' work is much worse and dirtier.

There was a good crowd in the church tonight. I kept Lent badly this year, God forgive me. The English don't believe in anything and for them today is nothing more than the beginning of the Easter holiday—the day for eating hot-cross buns. Some of the Irish are as bad as them and, as I passed the pubs, I noticed that there were a lot of Irishmen in them. Today above any day of the year, I wouldn't like to touch a pint no matter how deep my longing for one.

Bert and I spent a long time talking when we went to bed. He's a decent, understanding poor devil and he went through a lot between the war and everything else. He tells me that there's nothing as good as the fine farming land down around his own place in Cambridgeshire and he has no regard at all for the farmers in these parts. He himself is the son of a small farmer but his father had to give up his place during the war and Bert has been working here in the hospital as a laundry-hand since he left the Army. Old soldiers understand one another anyway and I get more from Bert than from that rogue Nick up above.

An old man from Ballinrobe came into the ward on Saturday with a skin disease on both his arms from the elbows down. He is a Burke and after talking to him for a while I discovered that he had plenty of information about Captain Boycott* who lived in his part of the country long ago. Burke has been here since he was twenty but, to listen to him talking, you never think that he had left home at all. He spent his whole life navvying and that is still what he's doing though he's getting a bit long in the tooth for that work now. He has been in every part of this

* The actions of his oppressed tenants towards him gave the word 'boycott' to the English language.

18

country and I could listen to him for ever talking about the 'pinchers'* with whom he spent some time working.

When the doctor came in the afternoon, I was sent round the patients with him as there was no trained nurse available. We went round the lot of them and when we came to the man from the County Mayo, the doctor had a bit of a chat with him. As we left him, the doctor said to me:

'Notice how tense he is? We must see if we can find out what's worrying the poor fellow.'

It seems that worry or some form of mental anguish produces this disease in people and, if they can succeed in ridding themselves of the psychological disturbance, the illness clears itself up quickly enough. I surmised, however, that there was nothing of that nature wrong with Burke and that it was only the lack of ease that poor people back in Ireland have when talking to doctors and suchlike, particularly when they're not used to them. I had noticed the same thing earlier in the day when the sister in charge of the ward came along and spoke to Burke. I was going to mention this to the doctor but I thought it would be out of place for the likes of me to be teaching the man his business and I let the opportunity pass. All the same, the servant often sees a lot that the master doesn't notice.

There's a very nice young boy in this ward also. His name is Nicholas Dimidvik and he comes from the Ukraine. You'd think he was from Connemara to listen to him talking. He left home when he was eleven and he has never been back there since. He spent some time in the concentration camps at Buchenwald and Dachau. Like most of the other D.P.'s that I met since I came here, he's not too keen at all on this country and, like the rest of them also, he's always complaining. The Italians aren't like that at all—those that are here in the hospital at all events. The Italians exult because they have left hardship and poverty behind them at home. Wouldn't you think now that the Poles and the Ukrainians had as much trouble? But the Italians are always lively and gay while the others are dour and gloomy.

I went to Confession tonight and I walked for a while around town afterwards. There's always a lot of people knocking

* Pincher: a labourer.

around here on Saturday night—going from pub to pub. They don't drink as much as the Irish do, but they make so much noise and talk that you'd think they were doing the devil and all. That's their way, I suppose, and it's not for me to find fault with it.

You couldn't help noticing the fine women here, their numbers and their beauty. There are more blondes here than you'd ever see in Ireland but redheads are very few and far between. A lot of them have black hair but it hasn't got the blue-black quality that you get in Ireland. One thing I noticed since coming here—that you'd know an Irish person easier than anyone else. They usually have curly black hair and high reddish cheek-bones but even without these traits you can pick them out easily—except for the odd person.

To bed early.

*Easter Sunday*. I borrowed a bike this morning and went to first Mass so that I was able to be back on duty at half past seven. The man from Ballinrobe is getting worse and he told me that he didn't sleep well last night. He can't stop scratching his hands and that's not good for him. He had never spent a night in hospital before this and I think that it worries him to be here at all. I took away his clothes today to store them until he'd be leaving. The poor devil, he had nothing but a pair of corduroy breeches, hobnailed boots, a jacket and a cap. Isn't it little good all the big money he got since the war did him when he hadn't a penny to face the bad times with?

Mr. Gardiner was very elevated today, whatever the cause, and he started singing a bit at dinner. It was great of him to do it, I think. He stayed in good form through the afternoon while his wife was visiting him. She said: 'That's my own puir Jock back to his old self again, singin' and laughin' like he used to do before he got bad. Och, we'll no feel till you're back home again now, my puir wee lamb.'

But she's mistaken, I'm thinking. She was no sooner gone than he got gloomy again and he didn't speak for the rest of the day. The nice little nurse from Sligo tells me that he's the patient the doctor has the least hope for, whatever the reason is.

I thought to get away tonight without Nick knowing but he was watching me too closely and I had only got to the gate when he came up to me. I hadn't much money left and, however little it was, I wanted to spend it in my own way without anyone urging me from this pub to that pub unless I wanted to move myself.

That's the way Nick is—he's no sooner settled down in one pub than he wants to move on somewhere else. He's quarrelsome, too, and he thinks that because he's Irish he has to be challenging people. I was always easy-going enough but I'm afraid that if this young buck is hanging around me too often I'll have to take steps to defend myself. He nearly started a real fight tonight in the *Criterion*. The way it was, we were going down to the Gents—in this pub you have to go downstairs to the lavatory—when Nick got sick and started vomiting when we were only about half-way down. A young English chap, a fine cut of a man, was coming up past us and he said civilly enough:

'Had too much, then? Silly boy.'

Nick turned on him straight away and spat:

'Who are you calling—eejit.'

The boy got annoyed at this and not without reason though he probably didn't understand a word of what Nick had said even though the words had been addressed to him. There would have been a right row between them but for my intervention, though when that happened Nick was more inclined to attack me than the other fellow. I was pretty well fed up with the whole affair by this, however, and if he had really started on me, there's nothing more certain but that he'd have got a right belting.

I'll stay far away from him for the future, for he's a complete bowsey.

I was off on Monday but, if so, it was little good to me for I had no money; and I still owed Bert that quid. All the same, the day was a good one and I had great gas with the Italians after lunch. Seven or eight of them were gathered together down in the club-room singing their native songs and I'm telling you none of them were in the slightest bit shy. I'm picking up an odd word of Italian here and there such as *Che ora e*? *Quando tu fini lavore*? and other phrases like those. I think that anybody that knew a bit of Latin would find it easy enough to learn Italian and, like German, it's not all that foreign to anyone that speaks English. The other languages that are spoken here, Ukrainian and Polish, are not in any way related to western European languages, so far as I know, although an odd word here and there bears a resemblance to certain words in Irish.

Bert invited me out to the New Theatre tonight and I hadn't the heart to refuse. So out I went with him. I didn't care for the show all that much—dry old chestnuts and stupid little sketches. But bad and all as it was, there was worse to come. The curtain came down for a short interval and the violinists started off with a loud screechy kind of music that would have been enough to set the dogs themselves off. Suddenly, then, up went went the curtain and what faced us there on the stage but five or six naked women—oh! I tell you that they hadn't as much as a bit of thread on them, the rips—and each of them looked as if they hadn't had a bit of food for about six months. They stood there for a short while without as much as a sound from them, and all the time, the bandit of a manager was holding forth in a meek respectful voice about the beauty of womankind since the beginning of time—about Helen of Troy and all that— pretending that he was engaged in something noble and artistic when all it was, in fact, was a despicable method of enticing people in to spend their money.

Bert was thoroughly satisfied with the night and I didn't like to say that I by no means felt the same since he was such a decent fellow. But it will be a long time before I'm inveigled into that damned theatre again.

Doesn't a body become very used to a place quickly enough?

A fortnight ago today I arrived in this place for the first time but, short and all as the period has been, I've got so used to the work and the people that I imagine that I've been here for years. I had a fine long letter from my mother giving me all the news and that's what set me thinking about how quickly I've got used to this kind of life.

Burke was a bit improved when I went into him this morning

and the doctor is talking about letting him home soon. 'Well, I think we could nearly let you go home, Mr. Burke,' Dr. Coles remarked to him on his round this morning. 'You seem to have cured yourself.'

As we moved a bit away from him, the doctor said to me. 'I wish I could get at the reason for his tenseness. I had a little chat with him yesterday but couldn't seem to find out anything much."

Well, I said to myself, I might as well give him my own opinion whatever he says about it.

'Well, I think I may be able to throw some light on it, Doctor,' I said. 'You see, at home in Ireland a great many of our people were brought up somewhat in awe of professional people like yourself and they never feel quite at ease in the presence of doctors, lawyers and other like people. I've noticed it often and in my opinion that's what is wrong now. Mr. Burke is only tense when yourself or the sister is around.'

At first, I thought he was going to tell me that he knew about these things better than I did but, on my soul, he didn't. He was indeed very interested in what I said.

'H'm, how interesting,' he replied. 'Well, it seems as though we go to the other extreme in this country, because there's rarely any great respect shown to a doctor here and half of my patients try to tell me what to do.'

Poor Burke was as excited as a child when he was told that he could go off home. He didn't like the hospital and hadn't been at ease at all since he was admitted. Maybe the cement or the diesel oil from the mixer was the cause of his skin trouble for they say that building workers often come in with the same ailment. That other poor man, Mr. Gardiner, was in a bad way today and he didn't want anyone to come next or near him, even to make his bed or do anything like that.

Nelly, the girl from Sligo, was telling me this afternoon that it won't be long now till she marries and goes off to Canada where a lot of her in-laws are already. Wouldn't you think, now, that it was a poor thing for a nice little girl like that to be married out in that place to a foreigner, and not one of her own people anywhere near her? They say that the Lithuanians and the Poles stay closely together when they emigrate to Canada,

23

C

for there's not all that much welcome for them out there. Anyway, I sincerely hope that Nelly will be lucky wherever she goes for she's a really decent girl. She has been very good to me ever since I came here and there are times when I think that it wouldn't be all that much trouble to entice her from her man, if I went about it properly. But, alas! it will be a long time yet before I can begin to think of anything like that; and, even then, maybe I won't come across the likes of Nelly.

I was finished at five and I wrote letters after tea. I sent off a good long one to my mother, telling her about life here and the price of clothes and all that kind of thing—stuff that she would be interested in; and I wrote off to the old Fenian also. I won't send off that letter until Thursday when I'll be able to send him the price of a drink with it.

*Whit Sunday.* This is my last day working in the hospital and sorry enough I feel about it. But, even so, I wouldn't stay on working for four pounds five shillings a week when help was needed so much back home. I was sorry to have to say good-bye to the patients and they felt somewhat the same as we all got on together very well. I learned that much about patients who suffered from skin diseases—that it does them more good that people should be gay and encouraging with them than that they should have all the ointments and tonics in the world. That is, of course, if the cause of their illness is psychological. If the disease was contracted from someone else or was contracted from contact with something infected, it is another story.

Indeed, any young lad without dependents could do worse than go and learn the business from start to finish and he'd always be sure of a good job as long as he'd live.

# 2

# Navvying with Mike Ned

---◆◆◆---

I hauled my bag off down to the lodging house that Steve Darby had recommended and di ty enough it looked after the cleanliness and airiness of the room I had in the hospital. The landlady offered me a meal but, when I saw it was spam that they had for tea, I said that I wasn't hungry.

I went off down town and felt kind of free having left the place above. I drank four or five pints of Guinness and mild in the *Cross Keys* before going to the dance in the Irish Club. The hall was overflowing and there were a good few strangers over from Corby there. I'd estimate that a third, or maybe half, of the crowd that comes here never gets out on the floor at all. They hang around the door chatting together or up at the tea counter and they're usually the finest looking men in the place whatever is the cause of it. Some lovely women attend the club, and, strangely enough, most of them go home after the dance unaccompanied.

Usually there's a game of pitch and toss outside the club when the dance is over, that or a fight; and the lads seem to be more interested in those pursuits than in the women. As soon as the boys start tossing, a couple of police come over and begin to move them on; but in a few minutes as soon as the police are gone, they start off again. One night I saw them with huge bets down and they didn't pay the slightest attention to the policeman who came across to remonstrate with them. What matter but they all had been a long time in this country and they knew well enough how much against the law it is to be laying bets, particularly in a public place.

Tonight, however, they weren't tossing the pennies after the dance; but there was a tough hard fight going on between a lad from the Meath Gaeltacht*, Ginger Folan, and Black Molloy from Leitrim. The Leitrim man had been taunting the Meathman all night and I had thought that the Meathman was frightened as he took so much without making any heavy weather of it. But the redhead was a stranger in town and he didn't know but that he'd have to fight a whole gang instead of just one man. When I found out what was worrying him, I said: 'God knows, we won't see you treacherously attacked; aren't we all from the same part of the country back home, after all?'

'God bless you, brother,' he said. Myself and Steve Darby would stand by him if it was necessary. He then told the Leitrim man that he would fight and the priest was sent for. A large crowd stayed after the dance to look at the fight and they were well satisfied for there was a good exchange as long as it lasted. They were about equal in size and weight. They fought without slipping or any other awkwardness and walloped one another as hard as they were able—fighting as good as any two boxers. Folan wasn't knocked down even once but he floored his opponent three times in a row; the lad stayed down the third time with the blood pumping out of his nostrils.

Folan was very upset about all this for he had come into the dance without any thought of trouble and I think he supposed the Irish here were against him because of where he came from. There is enmity between those who were given new holdings in County Meath and those who had been there a long time—even in this country! He let a wild roar out of him and jumped up and called on anyone who wanted any fight to stand out. Nobody moved; and if he only knew it, there were plenty there looking on who were only too pleased at what had happened to Molloy. The priest lifted up the defeated man and took the gloves away from both of them.

* Gaeltacht: a district where Irish is the everyday language.

'Shake hands now,' he said, 'and go home like good Christians and don't let me hear that more of this happened out on the street.'

I've no comfort at all writing this in the boarding house, somehow, and I had to say to one of the lodgers in the end that I was writing an urgent letter home. But what harm? We'll have a great day in London tomorrow watching the hurling match between Galway and Tipperary.

I got a seat on the bus going to London on Whit Monday for the match without any trouble. Not as many travelled as they had expected. I had hoped to see Steve Darby coming towards us any minute but he didn't arrive and we had to move off without him. The morning was marvellous and we had a gay crowd in the bus that sang songs all the way down. I was more interested in the countryside for it was the first time I had been outside Northampton since I had come over. The driver of the bus didn't seem to be in a hurry and it was one o'clock by the time we reached London.

We had hardly time to get a bite to eat and to knock back a couple of drinks before it was time for us to be heading for Mitcham. As I went into the park, I thought for a moment that I was back in Ireland there were so many of our people there. There were people from every county in Ireland, I'd say, but naturally most of them sported the colours of Galway and Tipperary. I met so many of my old friends and old Army comrades that my head was almost spinning; and my right hand was wrung so much that I thought it would fall off. Some of the people I met were: Beaver Walsh, Red MacLoughlin, Johnny Connolly from Aran (he had just spent three months sea-faring between Greenland and Newfoundland on a Milford Haven trawler) Mag Ridge, Dolly John Pat Feichin and the daughter of Sean MacDermott and Brigid Thornton.

The game went well enough and as usual, Galway were away ahead in the first half but I'm afraid that Tipperary weren't slow to forge ahead after that. Jimmy Brophy was playing for Galway, and as they marched around before the game, I let a yell or two out of me but it was useless: he didn't see me. More than anything else I wished that he would see me and that he'd be telling the lads back in Renmore on his return that he had spotted me there but I suppose it's hard for a player to see any one person in such a gathering where there are thousands present.

After the game, we all went over to the *Swan* which was across the way but there were so many there that it was hard enough to get a drink at all. I saw more people that I knew and there was a man from Claregalway declaiming *Anach Cuain* as well as I've ever heard it with some of his friends encouraging him by shouting now and again: 'Up Annaghdown anyways.'

London must contain some of the finest men and women that ever came over from Ireland. In any event, I never saw so many fine handsome men and beautiful girls all gathered together in the same place before.

When we were all back in the bus and just as it was pulling out, who did I see but Mary Mulhall from Kilkenny whom I had loved once without her knowing it. I got the driver to stop and I jumped out and started to talk to her. She's now nursing in London and she's looking wonderful, God and Mary bless her. Her heavy blonde hair was as lovely as ever I remembered it and there was no diminution in the fine healthy colour in her two cheeks from other days. I couldn't delay too long with her there, much to my sorrow, but maybe that was just as well for I might have found myself falling in love with her again!

In we went to Hammersmith, a great Irish centre, and there the crowd dispersed. Most of them were teetotallers and they went their own way while the 'drunks' made straight for the pubs. We spent a couple of very nice hours there in the *Six Bells*, where all the Irish gather and I met Mike's family there— Stephen, Martin and Joseph. They were a fine crowd but then, that's Carna. The men and the women from there were elegant any day of the week.

We moved off to the dance in the Garryowen when the pub closed. Big as the hall was, it was full and I met as many there that I knew as I had met in Mitcham. The Irish in London, I'd say, have a great life, plenty of their own people all around them, galore Irish dances and somewhere to go every night of the week. I hope to leave Northampton and get work in London, if I can at all, for there's nothing to do up in that place. Wouldn't it be fine to be working down here when I'd meet my own old comrades all the time? It would be as good as being back in Renmore!

I slept nearly all the way back to Northampton.

Most of the men had their own woman going back with them, all but myself and one or two others. Now, if we were back in Connemara or in Spiddal, you can be sure that I wouldn't be without a nice little girl to see home at the end of a night!

It was as much as I could do to drag my body out of the bed next morning. I managed to get up, however, and off I went down to Regent Square to meet the man from Cornamona as I had arranged the previous day. Curran is his name but he's known as Mike Ned. We moved off down to Town Centre where we got on the wagon of the contractor that's doing this work in Towcester and away we went. We hadn't got the job at this stage but we went out 'on spec' and, thank God, we got the job. A lot of others came out looking for work also but some of them were sent away. I was lucky that I got a job so readily, especially as I didn't particularly look like a navvy at all—or not much.

We were sent off to the store to get tools—picks and spades and crowbars, and then we made our way down to where they were breaking the ground. The engineer had marked out a big square where Mike Ned and myself were set to work, excavating to a depth of four feet. Mike Ned has been on this work since he left school and it was worth while to see him using the pick and digging at the hard ground. I thought I was as good as him and I started off like the hammers of hell belting at the ground with the pick but for all that I did I might as well have stayed at home.

Mike Ned, however, showed me how to go about it properly—not to lift the pick too high and to hit in the same place always and not to be hitting haphazardly with it. I worked better after that and I tried hard because I didn't want to have any of the lads saying: 'What kind of a man is that that can't work like a proper navvy?' We worked away and when the first break came at ten o'clock I had blisters on my hands and my back felt as if somebody had been laying about it with a stick.

29

We got our tea out of a big bucket and every minute of the ten-minute rest was like heaven. When the whistle blew to call us back to work, it was as if a judge was sentencing me to death; it couldn't be avoided, however, and back into the hole went my companions and myself. I kept on doing my best and shovelling but, no matter what I did, I wasn't as good as the next man. When we had a certain amount done, Mike Ned told me to change around with him; he started working on my portion and he wasn't long tearing the stuff out. Just about then the ganger came round and he said:

'Good lads, ye're doing all right. Now would ye come up behind the mixer for a while?'

My heart sank at this for I had heard so much about the same malignant mixer that I had no wish at all to go next nor near it—until I was more experienced in the work at all events.

We went along anyway and what I was told to do was to shovel the sand into the hopper. Four men are supposed to work on a mixer of this kind—one driver who also throws in the bags of cement, one man who shovels in the sand and two others who shovel in the gravel—and indeed it's necessary to have the lot of them when you have a dumper or two taking the concrete away from the mixer as fast as it comes. Eight shovelfuls of sand to twice that amount of gravel and one bag of cement are the proportions laid down.

The job I had was no trouble and I could see that Mike Ned and the man with him were working much harder than I was. Shovelling sand is different from shovelling gravel; the man on the gravel puts in twice the effort. When I had worked a while at the sand, the man who was carrying the bags of cement came over and said:

'You're new to the game so I'll give you a break. Take over the bags, you, and I'll do the hard graft.'

I thanked him and did what he said but it wasn't long before I found out that the rogue had tricked me for heaving the bags was slavery compared with what I had been doing. One hundredweight was in each bag and, while the weight itself was nothing to me, for I had often carried as much, it was the devil and all to be doing it again and again without a break while the dust from the cement would choke the devil himself.

30

'The devil's luck to you,' said Mike Ned. 'Why didn't you stay as you were and not be such an eejit?'

He's a great worker, Mike Ned, though he's hardly there at all, as you might say. He's never idle for a minute and as soon as the hopper is filled, he starts piling the gravel up in a heap. Any time he got the chance, he came over and heaved a bag of cement for me. I don't know at all how I'd have got through the day but for his help. I was ready to fall by the time the dinner break came and only half the day was gone by then. We wolfed the sandwiches of bread that we had with us and drank a drop of tea. I'd have given my two eyes for a pint of milk at that minute if it could have been got.

I don't know how I got through the rest of the day. I'd be exhausted and as weak as a cat and then I'd gather enough strength to keep going for another while. Be that as it may, when six o'clock came and it was time for us to go along on the wagon that would bring us homewards, I was as happy as if I was being driven in the King's own car.

I spent the night at home.

I was hardly able to straighten my back next morning when I was getting up. Mike Ned was waiting at the corner and not a sign on him that he had done a stroke of work the day before.

Thanks be to God, they weren't concreting today and we were left by ourselves down in the hole digging. Three shillings an hour they're paying here and a bonus as well if we can earn it. I don't know what has to be done to earn the bonus but, as far as I'm concerned, even a bonus of five quid wouldn't compensate me for what I suffered yesterday on that damned mixer. I didn't find today half as long for we had a good bit of chat as the man from Cornamona yarned away about home all the time. The Irish he speaks is not the same as Connemara Irish but I'm familiar enough with his dialect because of the number of men from the north that I met in the First Battalion.

We all worked together in the one gang in the afternoon; there was a huge heap of clay to be shifted so we were all put on this job with two dumpers to cart the stuff out in. Lavelle from Achill and a big strong Austrian called Franz were filling one dumper with an old Irish 'pincher' and after a while the man from Achill told me to get up on the dumper and have a go at driving it. I felt a bit unwilling to do so to begin with but, however, up I got to see if I could make any kind of a fist of the damned machine. And, oh! brother, I had only got up and released the clutch or whatever the hell they call it, when off the machine went like the wind and me without a clue about how to stop it.

The lads scattered like flies as they saw me coming and on I forged like one of those impregnable tanks the Germans used to have. The engineer had little bits of wood stuck in the ground marking out the place where pipes were to go and where foundations were to be dug; but I rode over them and reduced them to dust. I managed to turn the steering wheel to the right then and I kept on going in a big wide ring until I came back to where I had started. I had done enough damage by then— sticks smashed, bits of the pipe shoved well into the ground and an old carpenter nearly killed only he jumped swiftly out of my way. The lads were in stitches of laughter at me but damned if I could stop the thing at all. In the end, all I could do was to run the dumper up on the huge hill of clay and, even then, the wheels continued to go around though the dumper moved no farther. I leaped down off it and stayed well away from the damned thing for the rest of the afternoon.

I wasn't half as tired this evening as I was yesterday. I went out tonight and drank two nice pints at my ease in the *King's Head*.

We were put on the bloody mixer again this morning, Franz, Mike Ned, myself and another man. I didn't find the work half as hard today. I'm probably getting used to it. The big Austrian is a right lad and he has a great smack for Mike Ned and myself. I don't think I ever saw a person as big as he is. He must be about six feet four inches tall and he has two hands on him that must be as big as the clutch pedal on the mechanical digger. He gets great satisfaction from listening to us talking in Irish and, every time an Englishman comes within hearing distance, he gives me a sign to start off on the Irish. He's living here and married since he was a prisoner of war but for all that he has no great regard for the local people.

32

When the bags of cement are being thrown into the hopper you have first of all to split each bag in two with the blade of the shovel and then empty each half of the bag. If you give a good strong blow with the shovel you'll split the bag across but unless the blow is strong enough, the thick paper bag won't break. Big Franz was watching me and any time I managed to crack the bag in one blow, he'd say: 'Goot, goot. You strong, mine brudder.' But, if I failed, he'd look peevish and say: 'No goot, Dawnny, you veak like English fellow, bloody fish and chip merchant.'

Mike Ned was in stitches at him and, indeed, I couldn't help laughing myself.

It's amazing how many Germans and Austrians that are living here now though few of them dislike the natives as much as Franz. To tell you the truth, I think, for my part, that the Germans and the English resemble each other more than they resemble any other nation. Of course, they're of the same stock and, naturally, that must have something to do with it. They understand one another better than either understand us but I've noticed that the Germans always seem to have great regard for us.

It was pay-day for most of the lads today but damn the penny those who had only started this week got. Like everywhere else here, you're a week in arrears all the time. But it doesn't matter; we can draw some money tomorrow and have it deducted from our pay next Thursday. A 'sub' is what they call this and it's customary for most of the men to get 'subs' as often as they can.

When I had my dinner eaten tonight, I sloped off down to the hospital to see if any letter had come for me. I got such a big welcome, God save us, that you'd think I'd emigrated to America. I got a bit lonely as I looked around the nice clean sitting-room and the great comfort on every side. There's a big difference between this place and the dirty lodgings I'm in at the moment.

But it's in the nature of things, of course, that you can't have it both ways and I suppose that I'd have stayed working in the hospital if I had been satisfied there. I was lonely enough leaving as I thought of Nelly over in America. I hope she does well and that she'll enjoy married life out there.

It's beginning to look as if there's no release for Mike Ned and myself from that mixer but it's great the way I'm getting used to the work. I'm hardly a week working with the shovel but my hands are getting hard already and I'm looking a lot healthier. I was growing too fat and lazy in the hospital, anyway, and if I'd stayed there much longer, I'd never have been able for hard work again.

We spent the last hour today down in the field unloading two lorries of pipes that had been delivered. We had great gas for a while with MacNally of Westport, jeering three young lads from County Monaghan. It seems they're not long here and, if what MacNally says is true, they're very cute, saving every penny and sending the money home all the time. Your man started off, saying that they wrote home like this:

'Dear Mother, I hope you got last week's money all right and that you put it in the post office straight away. This is a very big job we are working on and the foreman is very nice; he comes and has his tea with us just like an ordinary man. There are some cat Irishmen in this place, Mother, always drinking and fighting and trying to borrow money, but, as you say, your friend is your pocket and so we have nothing to do with them. Well, Mother, that's all the news for the present, writing again next pay-day, Johnny.

'P.S. Did the black polly calve yet?'

He had the boys driven wild and I'm thinking that they would have fought him but for the fact that they were afraid of him. I know MacNally for a while now and, to tell you the truth, he doesn't like to see too many Irishmen coming over here in case there wouldn't be enough work to go around in the end. He has been in this country for over twenty years and his memories of the depression have affected him so much that he can't believe that it won't occur again. But he's a decent man and, wherever he is, there's always a bit of fun.

There's a pair of oul' 'pinchers' on this job and they're a couple of queer birds all right. Both of them wear very old-fashioned clothes—moleskin breeches tied at the calves with a pair of 'yorks' (two pieces of cord), neckerchiefs and hob-nailed boots. I'm told that they don't stay very long in any one place and that they have walked the whole country. They pay no attention to anybody else and they despise the young that come across nowadays.

They call the young people greesheens and latchicoes. They'd prefer the devil himself to anybody that would ask them where they came from back in Ireland and, if you had enough devilment in you to ask one of them that question, the answer you'd get would be: 'A peeler* wouldn't put that question to me.' They don't go anywhere except to the pub and it's a long time since either of them stepped inside a church. For all that, they're very loyal to each other and what one of them has is shared with the other who hasn't got it. They have a marvellous knowledge of England and, indeed, of the whole of Great Britain and there's hardly a place, no matter how small, that they haven't been in. They doss down in the 'kips' or cheap lodgings where they can look after themselves exactly in the way Pat MacGill† described in what he wrote about the life of the navvies fifty years ago. I imagine that they'd be all right with you if you were one of themselves but they have no time for anyone who dresses up to go out at night. For themselves they were the same suit day in day out without changing.

Mike Ned was telling me about one of these people that were in Northampton some time before. The man was from the Spiddal area, a fine good-looking man and he was on the 'toby', as they call it, for many a long year, moving from place to place just as the mood took him. Anyhow, his people at home got news of where he was and one of his brothers came over to try to persuade him to come home. There was a place for him over there (like a number of them he had been well-reared) and the brother went off and bought him a good suit and all that and gave him so much money. That was all right but when the time came for them to catch the train for Holyhead, by God, the man that came over to bring the labourer back might as well have been trying to entice a cat to get into a curragh. Your man only laughed at him and he spent every penny the brother had given him as well as the price of the clothes which he sold straight away the next day.

It's hard to imagine why a person would like that kind of life

* Policeman.
† An Irish writer who had worked in Britain about the beginning of the century.

rather than living on his own little bit of land but, on the other hand, the wandering labourer hasn't a care in the world and there isn't a night that he goes without his drop of booze even if he's not working himself. What these men are looking for, so far as I can see, is plenty to drink and freedom to go wherever they want to. I suppose that that kind of life has its own attractions.

We got a 'sub' of five quid that will keep us going until next pay-day.

Some of the lads stayed working on Saturday until four o'clock but Mike Ned and myself knocked off at twelve. I had a bath on the way home and put on my Sunday suit before dinner. I went out then to have a look at the market.

I could stay for ages going round the same market; there's so much to be seen there between fruit, vegetables and goods of all kinds; and there's a book-seller that has all kinds of books going cheaply. As well as that, of course, I liked having a gander at the handsome well-dressed women doing their shopping—a look of comfort and well-being on most of them. You wouldn't see an old shabby coat or broken shoes on anyone and, whatever about rationing and other tribulations, there's a great sense of plenty among the young people that have grown up since the beginning of the war. They say that the working man is much better off now than he was before the war—which is to say that in those bad days before the war, a man could hardly buy a bob's worth of meat for himself in a week.

There's work for everyone in this country now, thanks be to God, and long may it last even if it is a result of a dreadful war. But God help our own poor country that has nothing in it now but unemployment and despair. Look at any Irish paper and what do you see but the grand ladies at Leopardstown Races— that or other grand people at some 'do' looking like penguins at the South Pole in their dinner clothes. But you never see a picture of a man with a large family who is on the dole or of the crowds making for Dun Laoire every living day. Those who could solve the whole question are blind to it—either that or they don't give a damn.

I wasn't very often in Dublin or Limerick but any time I was

I couldn't help noticing the numbers of poor badly-clothed people that could be seen. And if you look at my old stamping ground, Galway, you'll see plenty of signs of poverty. It is understood, naturally, that we can never be as wealthy as England but we're so far behind other countries such as Denmark that one can only conclude that something has gone wrong somewhere.

Pat the Tailor, a Corkman, came to where we were working and offered Mike Ned and myself a job laying water mains for the County Council. Two pounds five a day he's paying so we jumped at the offer. The work will be much harder, of course, but no matter: we'll have a go at it for a while anyway.

When we went to the hut to tell the clerk that we were packing up, he made a miserable song and dance about the whole thing.

'But you've only just started,' he said. 'You can't just keep starting and finishing on jobs like this all the time. Think of the trouble you put us people to.'

'That will do,' said Mike Ned. 'Just lick 'em and stick 'em.'

The stamps were licked and stuck on to our cards and we got our pay—such as it was which was little enough. The two of us went off to the pub then and we stayed there until closing time.

As we came out of the pub, a lorry arrived and we managed to get a lift on it to Northampton without any bother. We got in at the back and there was a big tough labourer there but we took no notice of him. We talked away among ourselves, about the amount of money we had and things like that and before we knew where we were we had landed right in the middle of town.

When we got off the lorry, the labourer was on our heels and he shot off a stream of Connemara Irish at us. We nearly fell through the floor, I need hardly say! To make a long story short, he asked me for a couple of bob. I couldn't very well refuse him as he had heard and understood every single word we had exchanged while we thought he was deaf to everything we said. I stuck my hand in my pocket looking for small change but, by God, I had nothing smaller than a ten-shilling note. I hadn't the guts to refuse him so all I could do was to give him that lovely half-sovereign. I wouldn't have minded at all if he had wanted it for something urgent and important but of course, he'd do nothing but spend it in the pub.

But, God knows, if it comes to that, isn't it what I'd do myself? Let him be; I won't miss it this time next year.

We went in to the *Jolly Smokers* and we had great crack for a while. Most of the Connemara people go there now and you wouldn't know but that you weren't back at home. Nearly every one of the men there have hob-nailed boots, corduroy breeches and big 'donkey' jackets and most of them speak Irish all the time. One oul' lad sang 'The Song of the White Strand' and a good job he made of it.

It doesn't do them any harm at all to pay you two quid five a day here. They get the value out of you all right. God knows a Corkman doesn't let the grass grow under him. Mike Ned and I spent all day filling trenches and we didn't get much time for stretching ourselves. One thing, however—there isn't an Englishman anywhere near us; they're all our own people. Most of the lads are from Rosmuc and Carraroe, and only about three in our gang speak English, one of whom is a Latvian. It was like the old days when I was in the First Battalion where you heard nothing but Irish all around you. The men on this job are all very tough, working away there like horses; but it seems that they are all nice lads. I know some of them from an old date.

We're on the main road at the moment but the pipe-line goes through gardens and farms as well. You wouldn't be in the same place two days in succession on this job, we heard. You could be here today while tomorrow you'd be miles away depending on how Pat felt like moving you around—that or the actual demands of the job. He didn't say much to us today but it seemed to me on a few occasions that he was taking my measure as he looked at me from under the peak of his cap. Well, let him! I can do no more than my best.

I nearly fell out of my standing laughing at the oul' fellow from Cork who was working with us filling the trench. The poor devil, he was delighted to be beside someone who was satisfied to talk English to him—his heart was broken with the Irish since he started on this job. He was one of the most talkative men I ever came across—leaving aside some of the bucks that are always holding forth down there at Hyde Park Corner. And the outlandish talk that he went on with! What matter but that he meant every word of what he said. Little was troubling him but the number of Irish who were losing their faith over here. His brother's daughter was coming to no good in London, if you could believe him:

'Yerra, boy, I calls on her there lately to remind her of her obligations and she only laughed at me. Coming out of the bath, she was. "There you stand," sez I, "with your hair half-wet, washing and batting and drifting away from the rites of the Church".' I'm not sure that he didn't think that there was some connection between bodily cleanliness and loss of faith!

Floods of chat were pouring from him the whole day and, in the end, Pat the Tailor wasn't slow to notice that he was keeping the men idle. I'm afraid the poor man won't last jig-time here on this job. At last, Pat sent the two of us way down the field, well away from the other men. We had plenty to do down there, deepening a trench, but nothing would do this devil but to lean on his shovel and gossip away about anything that came into his mind.

'Wot do you think of the English, boy?' he said. I replied that I couldn't answer a question like that off the cuff but he didn't give me any chance to develop my point.

'Tyrants and robbers, that's wot they are, boy. Look at wot Cromwell did back yonder, boy. "To hell or to Connickt," sez he, and he drives all our ancestors from their rich lands an' their castles back into the mountains and boglands an' that's why we're all over here today working for John Bull.'

I was going to say to him that it was a bit ridiculous to be putting the blame for the state of Ireland today on whatever happened over 300 years ago but I let it go with him. When the lorry came in the evening to take us back home, out gets Pat to see what we had done. I'm afraid that we won't be together tomorrow.

Mike Ned and I went off to the pictures tonight.

'There was neither sense nor meaning to that picture.' he

D

remarked as we came out and he rubbed his hands together. What matter only he had been fast asleep through the whole picture!

We were in two minds this morning about what to do—whether to stay at home or go to work—for it was lashing rain and didn't look as if it would change. We got into the wagon anyway in the end (the job is over twelve miles from the city) but it was pouring down on us inside there. Ray O'Sullivan was pretending that we were sailors in a storm, roaring every now and again: 'Hold it, you devil, hold it, I say,' and other sayings that the Connemara boatmen have but that I know nothing about. When we got to the end of the journey, Pat was there before us and not looking all that well-disposed.

'There was no point in your coming along this morning, lads,' he said. Someone remarked that it might clear up after a while.

'Well, do as you please,' he said, 'but if you start, you'll have to stick it out until evening whatever about the weather.'

We were certainly in two minds then. None of us wanted to get drownded wet but at the same time we didn't want to lose the day's pay (there's no 'wet-time' money on this job). In the end, we decided to start so there we were digging, carting and preparing places for the pipes. By breakfast-time, no one had a dry stitch on him and we were disgruntled accordingly.

On this job, we all go into Towcester for the tea; we're all so dispersed that this is the most suitable thing to do. No sooner had we had our tea, however, and were feeling a bit more civilized that the rain started coming down heavier again. Soon enough Pat came to get us out again but it was no use—not a man stirred. That made him pretty annoyed and when every man started to ask him for a 'sub', he was fit to be tied. Those of us who needed it, however, got it from him in the end and as it was after ten o'clock by then, the lot of us moved out of the café and into the pub, every man jack of us.

The Sullivans, the Greallishes, Colm the Tailor, Paddy Walsh, Mike Ned and myself were all there and we had all the time in the world before us. When closing time came, we bought a half-dozen each and moved up to Martin Connery's

house. Martin is an in-law of Sean's and his wife Maura gave
us all a great welcome. I got great satisfaction from that part of
the day—the whole houseful of us there and not a word of
English being spoken: nothing but the best of Connemara
Irish. A lot of songs were sung: 'Return, O My Darling,' 'My
grief that I'm not a white duck', 'Rise up, gallant Sweeney' and
I don't know how many others and when Barney came with the
wagon to take us home, he had a lot of trouble getting us out of
Martin's house.

The weather is good, thank God, but the ground is terrible
after the rain. We were filling trenches out in the country a
good bit away from where we had been the previous couple of
days—Ray, the 'pincher', Mike Ned and myself. It was very
hard work for the clay piled along the top of the trench had
turned into mire and kept sticking to the shovel. Even a saint
would swear the way big dabs of putty clung to the blade no
matter what you did. We worked away for a while but it was
unsatisfactory not making much headway and it wasn't long
before the oul' fellow started off:
'Yerra, isn't it a queer world, too, boys, when you think of it
right. Here are we pulling and dragging from wan day to the
other and wot for? Just so that a boss can roll around in the
lap of luxury, winin' and dinin' and indulgin' in all manners
of idle pleasures, mixin' with the cream of society and going to
the opera. Yerra, 'tis enough to make wan a Communist, boy.'
As I envisaged the men we were working with doing all
those things, I nearly burst out laughing. They'd be far more
satisfied looking at a boxing match or drinking pints in *Ward's*
in the West End. But there was no point saying this to the poor
oul' fellow. He had an unconquerable imagination that had
little regard for fact.
About dinner-time, when there was no sign of Pat coming to
take us along to the café, we began to get a bit worried. We
were a long way from any place where we could get a drop of
tea or a bite to eat—and a dog wouldn't eat the spam sandwiches that we had brought from the 'digs'. Mike Ned was the
worst off for he's a devil for tea and if he had to get through the
afternoon without a drop, he'd nearly die. Pat had done the

same thing many a time before on men far out in the country
if he was any way busy. Work must come first, Pat would say.

He didn't come but, if he didn't, we weren't left without
something to eat and drink. An old farmer who was passing
by took pity on us and brought us up to his house. We went
with a will. And, fair play to himself and to his good woman,
they gave us plenty of lovely tea and home-made cake. But the
oul' 'pincher' nearly shamed us all as we got into the kitchen.

'Yerra, ma'am, we're really grateful for your hospitality.' he
said; but he couldn't say that and be finished with it. 'We holds
no personal grudge against the English as people, ma'am, it's
their policy we dislikes. Yerra, sure the common people are all
the same all the world over. Weren't yourselves, or your ancestors, anyway, trampled on like us by Cromwell and all the other
tyrants?'

I'm afraid Cromwell and history have hit the poor man so
hard that he can't leave them for a minute out of his conversation. Well, when we had eaten plenty, we got up to leave.
The farmer and his wife were mesmerized by the oul' fellow;
I'm almost certain they thought he was crazed, if not a real
lunatic. You could see from their eyes that they were worried
and I think they were half-sorry that they had brought such
outcasts in at all.

It's certainly I that was grateful when the oul' fellow was
across the doorstep but, by God, didn't he turn again and spout
out more of his words of wisdom at the old couple:

'The blessing of God on ye now, tanks a million! Isn't it
grand to see the common people surmounting the barriers of
race and religion and comin' together like true brothers.
Good-bye to ye now.'

'That you may be seven times worse off this time next year,'
ground out Mike Ned at him through his teeth.

'Wot did I say wrong, now?' said the oul' fellow, amazed
that we should be annoyed with him. 'Sure I was just tryin' to
establish friendly relations with them people and showing them
the Irish are not the barbarians they tink.'

There was no point in being at him. We got another 'sub'
from Pat at knocking-off time. I'm afraid we'll have little
coming to us on this week's pay-day.

We had great crack today for a while. We were out in the field and, as it was lashing rain, we had to get under the shelter of the ditch like Raftery did long ago round about Headford. There was a good crowd of us all together there and, as happens at times, we began to talk about life. I said, at all events, that our life on this earth was like that of the butterfly, it was so short; and then I suggested that we should suffer more consciously for the sake of our souls.

'On my soul, Danny, son, I think we've enough trouble and hardship in life as it is not to be adding to it,' said Martin Connery.

'By God, you're wrong,' said Paddy Walsh. 'Danny's right. Everyone should be harder on himself for his soul's sake.' Paddy was joking, of course.

That was enough for everybody else. Each man tried to surpass the other in describing the penances he was thinking up for himself.

'Wouldn't it be a good penance to be banging your head off the wall,' said Colin.

'Or if you held your breath in until your lungs were almost bursting,' said Ray.

'That, or you could shave with an old rusty razor in cold water,' added Tom.

'Yerra, none of them things would be like eating spam every day of your life.' said Mike Ned. And, right, enough watching him as he said these words, you could see that would be much worse for him than to be sitting on the red hob of hell itself.

There's no doubt at all but the people of Connemara are the best people in Ireland for having fun; and it's not the first time I've said that.

We had to go off home at dinner-time as the rain was too heavy to be out working in. We had time to have a drink in the *Rodney* before it closed.

Mike Ned and I went to Confession tonight and it was badly needed. We went to the pictures afterwards and ate a fistful of fish and chips on the way home.

Holy Communion this morning, thank God. Sunday is the day we like best here in Northampton. All the Irish gather here in the club after Mass—men, women and children. Tea is drunk, cards are played, work and sport discussed, mothers hold forth on the great things their children have done, friends and relations enquire about things at home from one another, Irish papers are sold and read, boys run around playing 'tig' and the accents of every county in Ireland can be heard in the place.

We had a bad dinner today—a huge dab of that rotten Yorkshire pudding bang in the middle of the plate. I don't know from Adam what it's supposed to be for, but the English go mad for it. God be with the bacon and cabbage at home with potatoes like balls of flour and where would you leave the mug of buttermilk? The landlady was drunk again today as every Sunday and abusing her unfortunate husband from time to time. They're a strange race, the English, no doubt about it.

I walked around town for a while after dinner. Mike Ned went asleep. Nothing affects me so much, I think, as seeing the little groups of Irish walking aimlessly around town every Sunday evening with no interest in anything at all, the creatures—only waiting for the pubs to open. For myself, I knew a little bit about this country before I came over, as a result of my reading and I take an interest in a lot of small things that the majority of these lads wouldn't bother about. But it's hard enough on young Irishmen who were reared out in the country to have nowhere to go on their day off except the pubs. It's small wonder that we are getting a bad reputation over here.

I read more of *Everlasting Man* after my tea. I'm afraid that there's little more in G. K. Chesterton half the time but a lot of smoke to blind himself and his readers. In any difficult or involved question that he starts to discuss, he draws on his hosts of paradoxes and, suddenly, he resolves the question to his own satisfaction. Anyhow, I don't see how any man who spent as much time as he did in the *Cheshire Cheese* could be all that deep a thinker. He'd understand feeling but he'd have to much regard for the way he was feeling. He'd be more human, more kind, perhaps, and he'd probably have an honest philosophy that would suit life around him; but, as for expecting me to depend on him to solve for me the great questions that preoccupy the human race, 'Ah, good morrow, Jack,' as the man said long ago.

I'll have to dry my working clothes for the morning or I'll get my death out of them.

# 3

# Stanford in the Vale

———◆◆———

*Monday, 1.12.1952.* In the *White Hart* in Acton Town, Mike
Ned and I met Peteen Lowery and we got a job from him
without any bother. Peteen is very strong now—plenty of
lorries and lots of men working for him. He's sending us up to
Berkshire and we'll be able to live in a camp there. But he
didn't let us go without well wetting our lips and we had great
crack for a time there with him. He is from Cornamona (the
same as Mike Ned) and another man from the same area was
with him. This was Jermyn Patch Nelly. He had been in
England for more than twenty-eight years but to see him standing there at the counter with his old dudeen* in his mouth and
talking away in Irish, you'd never know that he had been away
from home at all. But that's always the way, of course, those
who have been longest from home are those who have most
regard for their native background and traditions.

It's wonderful how Lowery got on since he came here. He
was only a navvy like the rest of us until he started up on his
own and now he has a contracting business almost as big as
Murphy over there in Finsbury Park. We said good-bye to him
at last and what do you think—didn't he give us a quid each
into our hands before we left. A generous man, God bless him.

We were ready then to set out for Stanford in the Vale in

* Smoking-pipe—usually a clay pipe.

Berkshire but nothing would do Mike Ned but to go across to
Camden Town to see if any of the lads from Rosmuc were
knocking around there. He hadn't stopped talking about them
since we left them back in Northampton. Mike Ned is a very
gentle person but he is also very headstrong and you might as
well be talking to the wall as trying to give him any good
advice.

In the heel of the hunt, of course, we didn't get out of London
at all and we finished up blind drunk in the *Black Cap* with a
crowd from Connemara. We got shelter for the night in
Rowton House in Camden Town. My God, you never saw such
a place. It was like a large barracks or prison, the number of
small bare cells that were in it. There was nothing wrong with
the beds, however and I had a great sleep even though I felt a
bit nervous about some of the 'residents' that I saw as I was
dozing off. A worse-looking crowd you wouldn't find anywhere.
Two and threepence we paid for the 'kip'.

Bad cess to Mike Ned, anyway, he wouldn't come to Berkshire with me when the time came. He'd stay around London
until his money was gone and then he'd mooch back to Northampton. Well, so be it; I'm through with him.

I had a long journey by bus and train and reached my des-
tination as night was falling and the snow was coming down. I
got to the camp and looked for the Irish speakers there—they're
all Connemara men who are working for Lowery here. The
others are working for Higgs & Hill who own the camp.
Lowery is only the sub-contractor.

The Irish language is a great help at times even though people
do run it down. When I found the man in charge of Lowery's
employees, I gave my story to him in English and didn't he tell
me that there wasn't any room for another man, no matter
what Lowery said. I was in a right fix then not knowing what
I'd do next until I heard someone inside the hut holding forth
in Irish. I stuck my head in and let fly at them a fine stream of
Irish. And what do you think your man did? He brought me
straight into the room and gave me as big a welcome as ever
I got!

'What the hell didn't you speak Irish to me?' he said. "Sure, I

couldn't know that you were one of ourselves!' I got my job
then with a heart and a half.

I went to bed early as I was tired after the journey. There
wasn't a spare bed in with these lads but I got one easily enough
in another hut with a crowd from every corner of Ireland.
They're a decent enough crowd but you'd think they were a
bit afraid of me (bad as I was) on account of my being thick
with the Connemara men. And maybe that's all to the good for
with that kind of support, they wouldn't be inclined to pick on
me so much.

We were stiff with the cold on the journey (about twenty
miles) to where we were working at the American Air Force
Camp at Brize Norton. Higgs & Hill have plenty of work going
on here but what we have to do is to lay underground cables.
There was no fear that we wouldn't be in form for work, it was
that cold, and the shovelling wasn't long heating us up. The
foreman was from Derrynea and most of the lads were from
Shanafesteen, with three or four from Lettermore.

When we went into the canteen at dinner-time to get a bit
to eat, I had a chance to seeing some of these all-powerful
Yanks and, mind you, I wouldn't think all that much of them.
To begin with, they're like school-boys the way they hog sweet
cakes and bottles of 'pop', where Irish soldiers would be looking
for pints of porter. And another thing, they've a stupid, almost
childish way of playing together without any of the manliness
that you get in the soldiers of the First Battalion back in Galway.
I still get lonely when I think of those fine strong men that I
spent the best days of my life with.

The camp is not any way expensive. Seven-and-six is charged
for the bed (stopped from your pay) and meals, which you pay
for yourself, are to be had in the canteen. You can live easily on
fifty bob a week, and even including the other charge, we're
a damned sight better off here than we'd be in 'digs' in some
towns. Some of the lads—the Connemara men in particular—
prepare their own meals in the huts but the authorities are very
much against this practice. 'Shackling up', this is known as. I
was talking to three men from Leenane tonight and they were
telling me that this is by far the cheapest way of looking after

yourself. They are very careful and they are able to save up to
ten pounds a week.

A decent enough crowd is in the room I'm in. There's one
huge man there—Corky he's called—and he's a great man
altogether. He gets out there in front of the stove every night
and starts spouting out of him on every subject you could think
of. He left Ireland when the Treaty was signed* and has never
gone back. Some breach of the peace that happened at that
time is responsible for his long exile, if it's true what I'm told.

We worked hard today hauling the cable. The same work,
indeed, is very hard on a cold frosty morning, grabbing a huge
cable and hauling it as hard as you could. Sometimes, as the
slack fell away from us, my ribs were nearly broken. There are
ways of making this work easier—to put little rollers under the
cable—but the lads didn't think this worth bothering about.
There's a strong man here known as Big Bartley and it's great
sport to watch him, he's so fine and handsome. He has hands on
him, God save us, that are as big as shovels and he has two
bright eyes in his curly head that are always dancing with life
and vigour. Bartley would spend his time amusing other
people, dancing and whistling, but they say that he's not such
fun when he has a drop taken.

Two pounds a day we are being paid here which is not bad
when you consider how few hours we work at this time of the
year. The little hut was like Heaven when we got back in the
evening for we were frozen with the cold. We had fine orations
from Corky on Betrayal and Betrayers, on Michael Collins,
Lloyd George and the rest. He held forth for a bit on the
excellence of the Communists; but I don't think that he has
any interest in them except that he feels that the lads would be
afraid of him if they thought he was one of that crowd. In his
heart, he's a decent poor man who can't live without an
audience.

I was talking to an 'intellectual' going out in the lorry this
morning. He's from Rossaville and he spent some time at
Galway University. Seeing that it was seldom I met a learned
man in this country, I started asking him about a few things that

---

* The Anglo-Irish Treaty of 1921.

I wanted to know about but, by God, he was hardly any more educated than I was myself. Oh, as far as Latin, Grammar and Arithmetic were concerned, they were all at the tip of his tongue but, beyond that, it seemed that his learning didn't help him to have more understanding of the life around him or of his work-mates. He's working on the shovel like the rest of us. As far as I can make out, he got nothing from his time at the University beyond a dislike for the lads he's working with and a deep-seated reluctance to speak Irish.

I spent a good part of the day behind a hangar talking to a Texan. He knows nothing at all about cowboys or Red Indians, I'm afraid.

As I went asleep tonight, the silence was broken with shouting and screaming, dreadful cursing and the noise of heavy blows. It was the Connemara men and the people from Dublin. They've been fighting this many a day.

I stayed off work today to go to Mass and, now that I think of it, it's the first time I've seen this place by daylight as I'm usually gone by early morning and it's dark by the time I get back in the evening. There was a fair attendance at the Mass but not as many as could be there were present. A special hut is set aside as a church here.

I took a turn about the village of Stanford in the Vale but there was little to be seen there and I came back to the camp without much delay. I read a bit more of *Days with Bernard Shaw*. I know that it's cheeky for the likes of me to find fault with Shaw or with those that praise him but I feel that it's a kind of adoration that some of them have for him; that there is nothing that he said, be it so ridiculous or outlandish, that isn't humbly and reverently written down by his followers. I threw it away in the end and started on a Westerner that brought back to me the days of my childhood. God be with those days and the innocence that went with them when black and white, right and wrong, were clearly defined as brave warriors and immaculate ladies reaped the harvest of their worthy deeds.

Well, Christmas is drawing near and I'm planning to go home if I can manage it at all. Corky himself is talking of going home this time. I told some of the lads that he had decided to recognise the Government of Ireland at last.

'Yerra, don't mind him,' they said. 'Corky would have gone home long ago except that he never had enough to get him back there. And he's never been on the "tack" as much as he is now.'

That was the end of my simplicity!

I am more than satisfied with the hut I found myself in the first night and I wouldn't leave it now for anything. I was invited today by the lads from Leenane to go in with them. I'm better off where I am, for they have closed minds—not like the crowd I'm with. We have some great debates and plenty of questions are discussed and the lads are not afraid of new thoughts; but the gang I'm working with, however, they'd prefer to do anything than to start any new train of conversation. None of them read the papers and they don't care at all about what's going on in the world.

Corky was at his best again tonight. He stood out there in the middle of the floor like an actor on a stage, telling a long story about some poor boy in the city of Cork that had to give up serving at the Altar because how the proud mothers of the other boys thought it was a come down for their sons to be seen in the poor chap's company. Corky went through all kinds of actions while telling the story. He pretended to be the parish priest, a high-minded proud man explaining to the poor outcast that he was grateful for his past services but, well there was this and there was that. When he came to the part where the little boy turned to leave the door of the priest's house, he put so much emotion into it that he nearly had all the lads crying.

Then, suddenly, he changed his voice, a black look came on his face, he hit the table with his fist and declaimed in a loud tough voice (and I remembered a short story by Sean-Padraic O Conaire* that I had read years ago): 'That little altar-boy is a grown strong man today. He is a great sinner and it's a long time since he crossed the threshold of a church. The evil tongues of other people always produce a bad result.'

As Geordie said to me afterwards, it would be all right if Corky was anyway trustworthy but he likes to add to and

* A Gaelic novelist and short-story writer.

embroider his stories so much that you can be sure that what you heard one night would be seven times better when you heard it a month later.

If the walls in the jakes here in the Yankee camp can be taken as guides, it seems that plenty of the soldiers think that the war between the States is still on; the same walls are plastered with slogans where they threaten death and destruction on each other. All sorts of evil are attributed to the Yankees by the Southerners while, if the other side is to be believed, there isn't a people anywhere else as sinister or as iniquitous as the Rebels. To tell the truth, I was surprised at this for I had thought it hardly likely that the ordinary soldier would either know or remember any of that kind of job; but it seems that this is not the case.

I had a great conversation with Colm Folan in the trench and managed to get him to debate a couple of subjects. He said that he would never go back to Lettermullen for love or money for he's ruined by city life; and, even now, he can hardly wait to go back to the Elephant and Castle where he keeps on rooms all the time and pays for them!

I thought the two hands would fall off me with the cold. The east wind was so piercing that it was like a butcher's knife stripping the skin off my bones. Some of the lads here can take anything; I'm thinking they must be made of iron. When I got back from the job to Stanford in the Vale, my feet were nearly falling off and I looked forward to my meal and to the heat in the hut more than anything else in the world.

A couple of cards awaited me in the canteen and it was only then that I remembered that it was my birthday. Well, I'm twenty-six years old today, thank God, strong and healthy without a care or a worry of any kind, and if I'm the same way this time next year, I won't be doing badly at all. From time to time, I think that it would be no harm at all to have a little girl to go out with at night but, on the other hand, it would be only a waste of time when I'm not serious about it. If I ever get married, I imagine I'll marry a girl from Connemara, for I like them the best—not only from the point of view of their physical beauty but also for the beautiful Irish they speak. But I'm a bit too young to be thinking of these things for a while yet!

We were a bit busy today crossing a road without a compressor to break the tarmac for us; but we worked away like the devil tearing and digging until the trench was ready (it was deep enough at this place) and the cable laid. A pretty little American girl came across while we were working on the road but like all the other children here, she had neither breeding nor good manners. It seems that it's true what they say about the Yanks—that they don't control their children. Fair play to the English, their families are well-trained.

Living over here is doing great damage to the Irish tongue of those who speak it as their normal language. For instance, today as an aeroplane passed overhead, one of the lads said (in Irish): 'What the devil keeps it up at all?' 'Oh! power agus* speed,' said Colm Folan (using the nouns in English). What matter but he could have used these simple words in Irish just as easily as he used the other trash. So they say: 'ringeail me suas†' or 'wireail me siar‡' or 'ag leveleail concrete§' and hundreds of other sayings that I can't recall now. If this continues I don't know what will become of the pure accurate Irish they spoke up to now.

But I don't know if these corrupt renderings are any worse than the ugly unintelligent modern terms that are being made up by the journals back home in Ireland.

Isn't it bad luck itself that you have to get up out of your nice warm bed these frosty mornings? As Mike Ned would say: 'What matter a day or two—but every bloody day?'

Fourteen pounds I drew today. On my soul, this is very good, the short days that are in it. Many is the time Mike Ned and myself were working under the eagle eye of Pat the Tailor up there in Northampton for the same money, if not less, and without the comfort we have here.

I stood outside the hut for a good while tonight looking up at the sky and at the ragged little clouds scudding across the moon and it came to me, not for the first time, that I would see exactly the same sight were I standing at home on my own

* And.
† Ring me up.  ‡ Wire me back.  §Levelling concrete.

threshold looking up in the same way. It's a funny thought, in a way, and wouldn't you think that there would be a kind of a tie or a bond between two people, one here and the other back in Ireland, both looking up at the moon at the same moment? Anyway, the air here tonight was as health-giving as ever I've known it and I could have stayed forever there inhaling it into my lungs.

The Camp Chaplain came around for a while selling Christmas cards and holy pictures and Corky offered him a slug of tea from his own can. By God, he drank it too and, if he was thought well of before, the respect for him afterwards was beyond all bounds. And what would you think of the bold Corky talking to the priest in as mannerly a fashion as you ever saw just as if he had never said a word against the clergy in his life—and he threatening death and destruction on the Church among many other things as long as I've been here!

It snowed heavily enough last night and it was up to our ankles as we came out of the hut in the morning. It was worse on the other side of Farringdon and we nearly went into the ditch a couple of times before we reached Brize Norton. We worked in the snow up to dinner-time but Tom Keady, the foreman, told us then that we needn't go out again.

A very nice man, this Keady, and very learned unlike most of the other lads here. He composes songs and I'm told that he won some prize or other in the Oireachtas*. I spent some time talking to him in the canteen but I got no real satisfaction out of it as the others were throwing crusts of bread all around us. I don't on earth know what that's in aid of—they're like children. That big curly-headed bull, Big Bartley, is worse than any of them bellowing and ranting all around him from morning to night. I never saw him look at a paper nor did I ever hear any intelligent word from his mouth.

We moved off home early as there was nothing we could do in the snow. I met an old lad from the Claddagh† back in the canteen of the camp. Moose Connolly they call him and, like a lot of the old boys that are with Hills & Higgs here, he's only

---

* The annual cultural festival of the Irish language.
† An old Irish-speaking district in Galway City.

passing the time until Christmas when he moves back to his own place in London. They're much to be pitied, these old men, spending the last days of their lives moving around from camp to camp and from room to room without a sinner to mourn them when they die a lonely death in some dirty, broken-down old lodging-house. They worked and they drank and they fought while they were there and now as their time draws near they have nothing to do but stretch their bones in some corner, turn their faces to the wall and wait for death.

Most of us were there in the hut as comfortable as anyone could be, some asleep, some sitting around the fire listening to Corky holding forth in his usual fashion, when we heard ructions outside and the door of the hut was kicked in fiercely. There in the doorway stood Big Bartley and he blind drunk, his two wild eyes jumping out of his head. He let a roar out of him and looked all around the room.

'Is there any —— from Dublin here?' he yelled. In English he spoke, of course, and not a man answered him. I'd have answered him myself but I was afraid to draw him on me.

'Is there any —— from Dublin in here?' he said again. 'If there is, let him stand out here till he sees what a Connemara man can do.' God be thanked, there was none of that crowd in the room and Corky told him that there wasn't.

'Yerra, come in ower that, me oul' skilleara, and have a jorum of tay; and don't be bothering yer fine head looking for them oul' jackeens' said Corky talking in the way he thought would suit Big Bartley.

Corky normally speaks in a very refined way with an Oxford accent or what he imagines is an Oxford accent. Big Bartley softened and in he came and sat down beside Corky and took a mug of tea from him. You could see nothing but fearful eyes staring out of the beds all around at the rogue and the little Englishman down below me was shaking with fright under the sheets.

Big Bartley got very kind towards Corky and the other lads sitting around the fire and he gave them cigarettes. Nothing would do him then but to give us a 'stave' of a song and, God bless us, the one he selected to sing—The Song of Captain Tim

O'Malley—I thought he'd never finish it. He got up and went away in the end and we were glad to see him go.

'Thank 'eaven, I ain't a —— Dublin Pateen or whatever you call them,' said the little Englishman, sighing with relief.

'There's nothing to be afraid of at all, old boy,' said Corky putting on the refined accent again. 'It's just a matter of knowing how to cope, and of understanding the dim recesses of the peasant mind.'

'Long years to you, Corky,' I said in my own mind, 'for it's you that's well able for anything.'

I went out to the job in the morning for I had been told that Mass could be had out at the aerodrome in the Air Force chapel. You would never have known from Big Bartley that he'd had a drop taken last night, he was that hale and hearty leaving.

We weren't all that busy; so as it came near Mass-time, myself and the lads from Shanafesteen moved off down to the chapel. It's a small wooden building and both the Catholic and Protestant worshippers use it. I had hoped to slip in unseen and to get a place well at the back but what do you think, didn't one of the Yanks grab me by the elbow and guide me up to the very top of the place. My old working clothes and hob-nailed boots looked so dirty and mean in there among the soldiers' neat uniforms that I signalled to my man not to bother—but that's all the good it did me.

When they went round with the collection plate (which they did twice), there was nothing but paper money on it and I had to part with two half-crowns so that I wouldn't be shamed altogether. The priest gave a little sermon that I found interesting—not because of the quality of the speaker for he hadn't got the gift of speaking—but for what I learned from it. He started by telling the congregation that they should be more loyal to their clergy and that it wouldn't shame them at all to address a priest as 'Father' while talking to him. It seems that some of them call the priest 'Mr.' which amazed me. He then said that they shouldn't be surprised to find that a priest could have a good car and things of that kind—that it happened frequently enough that it was the priest's family who gave him whatever he had. It was new to me to find a priest excusing himself, as you might say, for having these things and I was stunned to find an American doing it.

I found the afternoon very long as I had nothing much on hand but Tom Keady shortened it by telling us some fine stories. He had plenty of little stories that were very good—like the one about the man from the Joyce country* that saw a crab for the first time down on the strand. 'Look here, boy,' he said said to his companion, 'look here, come and see the giant spider!' The young fellows here, however, are not interested in that kind of thing and they think that Tom is off his head to be bothering with old traditional lore of the like. Drink, squabbling and big pay—that's all they want and the devil take anything else. When they come over here, they seem to lose the friendliness and the kindness that are the marks of the people of the Gaeltacht at home.

We went home early and I spent the night at my ease reading for the second time *Sick Heart River* by John Buchan. God be good to the day long ago when I read it for the first time and to the courage and the hope that I had then. I wouldn't believe then that I would be living anywhere else but in Canada when I grew up, married to a nice little French-Canadian girl with dark tresses and blue eyes and a nice foreign name such as Marie La Coutre or the like. We'd live by hunting and fishing and I'd now and again half-kill some Pierre and Jean-Baptiste just to show that the Irish were unbeatable. Youthful madness. But such dreams were lovely when life was grim and everything going against you.

When I left school and went to work in the mill, I was often depressed thinking of the unpalatable ordinariness that faced me labouring and pinching and scraping. That would be the time when I'd start dreaming and I'd have everything arranged to my satisfaction in a very short space of time. Another couple of years and I'd be trapping wild animals and selling their furs up there in the north of Saskatchewan. I'd be bold, headstrong, virile, tough and when the other hunters would bare their knives at me, I'd bare my teeth in a dangerous grin at them!

I little thought then that it would be behind a spade in John

* An area in Co. Galway.

Bull's land that I'd spend my life. If I had thought so, I'd have been fed up to the back teeth. But, to tell the truth, you could be in many places much worse than here. Everyone gets fair play in this country and, if anyone wants to advance himself, nobody at all will try to stop him.

I never experienced in my life any day as cold as today was. My two hands turned blue-black, they were so stiff as I was trying to shove the damned cable through the pipes. The pipes were down in a hole that was full of water and it was murderous to have to plunge your hands in the same water. God save us, it was the devil's own work. I got pins and needles in my palms in the end. Tom Keady and myself were on this job and we were just in front of one of the Americans' lecture rooms when one of them comes out and stands gawking at us. '——', he said swearing, 'What a deal! Why, I sure wouldn't wanna do what you guys are doin', not for a —— million bucks!' He had a Southern accent and I was thinking of asking him if the Ku Klux Klan were still going strong but I let the opportunity go by.

When we got back from work in the evening, there were two new bucks in the hut there before us. One of them was from Canada, a big blond fellow, while the other was from Grimsby, however the hell they teamed up together. Right from the start, we were fed up with them holding forth about all the places they had been in and all they proposed to do when they would have so much money saved. Even poor Corky didn't get a word in edgeways and he didn't like that one bit.

The Grimsby man started about religion. He said that the Catholic Church was pulling the wool over the eyes of half the people in the world. His authority for this talk was that he was half-Irish himself and had been baptised a Catholic. He hadn't any religion himself at all nowadays and he wanted to spread his own gospel. When he paused to draw breath, what do you think but my fine Corky started off on him defending the Church!

'My deah man,' he said in a superior but irritated tone, 'I wondah if you are aware that the Catholic Church has been the greatest instrument for good—despite its many faults—that the civilised—ah, world has known?' The Grimsby man tried to get in again but Corky had managed to get the floor and he couldn't be stopped. You could see the lads looking at him with respect and wonder in their eyes. He routed your man and saved the reputation of our little hut all right. But if your man himself had been a good Catholic and was defending the Church to his utmost, you can be sure that Corky would have attacked it as effectively!

We heard that the sub-contract might be finished by Christmas. If so, we'll have to look for work from Higgs & Hill—that is, if we want to remain on in the camp. That's what I propose to do anyway for I like the place well enough now and I'd rather come back here than go somewhere else where I'd have to start looking for lodgings all over again.

Big Bartley and Tom went for me this morning because I spoke to the Grimsby man while we were coming out on the lorry. It was the way he asked the driver for a lift out to Brize Norton, having missed the Higgs & Hill bus. He began to talk to me as soon as he got into the lorry and I could hardly refuse to answer him. After we had been talking for a while, Big Bartley let a roar at me: 'Why the hell are you getting great with that bowsie from Dublin?'

'Yerra, Bartley, he's not from Dublin,' I answered. 'He's from Grimsby.'

'They're all the same, all them devils,' said Bartley (and Tom started to support him): 'You shouldn't be talking to them at all if you're from Connemara.'

I didn't speak at all after that and, of course, Grimsby didn't know at all what we had been talking about (we had spoken in Irish); but if I could lay my hands on Tom some place where he hadn't his big friend to protect him, I'd kick him until he changed his tune.

When I got back from work, there was a letter from home waiting for me as well as one from my brother up in Northampton. Mike Ned had returned there, according to him, and was working on a little job in town where he wasn't too far from the café. What he'll be looking for now is plenty of tea to drink and damn the work. I'll have to write to the poor devil now. He tells me also that there is nobody from Connemara left in

Northampton since I came away from it. I don't know how Pat the Tailor will get on without those lads, to tell you the truth.

The Canadian gave us a turn on the mouth organ tonight and I must say that I have never before heard anyone play that instrument so well. He played plenty of cowboy tunes, such as 'Red River Valley,' 'Sierra Sue,' and 'Headin' for the Last Round Up'. He told us that he used to work in lumberjacks' camps in Canada and that a lot of the men there were great singers. He's damned good himself, anyway, and it's just as well, as the lads here will have more respect for him when they know he's a musician.

I visited the Leenane lads tonight and they didn't let me go back home on an empty belly. They gave me plenty of chicken and a huge mug of tea. They're looking after themselves, naturally; and although meat is supposed to be rationed, they can get what they like from the butcher as long as they have the money to pay well for it. Irish is only the second language of these boys from Leenane and English is what they mostly speak among themselves. Their English is not that good, for all that, though it's what they have always spoken: from the old people they heard the Irish. But even though they have no particular regard for Irish, they speak it much better than a lot that learned it with diligence and patience.

I've noticed this before about the Leenane lads and others from the English-speaking areas of Connemara, that no matter how long they stay in England their command of the language doesn't get any better. But as far as the men from Lettermore and Balladangan are concerned, people to whom English is as foreign as to any people from Europe, they manage to get along with it wonderfully and, if they have the wish, they soon learn to speak it as well as those who were born to it.

Maybe the reason for this is that English *is* a foreign language to them and they try to learn it as someone from France or thereabouts would—fully and perfectly. On the other hand, the man from Leenane or from Errismore who has been listening to English (of sorts) since he was born, doesn't think that it's necessary for him to have to learn it at all. So he goes through life saying things like: 'Did you went to the dance last night?'

or 'Fy so?' and not being a bit embarrassed about it at all.
Another thing, in the Gaeltacht, there is more of a desire for
learning and reading than there is in the Brae-Ghaeltacht* or
the Galltacht† in Ireland. I knew scores of men from Carna
who spoke the best of English although they only had the odd
opportunity of speaking it. From reading they acquired their
facility and, as a result, it's no wonder there were traces of
literariness in their conversation.

Today, we kept an eye out for Peteen coming with the pay
but in the end it wasn't him. Twelve pounds I got—I had
stayed away last Sunday, of course—and that's not bad seeing
the days are so short. But it was also confirmed that this job is
finished for a while anyhow until Lowery takes up the contract
again. So we'll be finishing up on Saturday night. What harm!
It's almost certain that we'll get work here from Higgs & Hill
after Christmas and, for myself, I'm determined to stay for a
good spell, if I can at all.

It started to rain then in the afternoon and Tom Keady was
trying to have what cable we had laid covered but it was useless
for him to expect to get anything done since the lads heard that
the job was almost finished. That's always the way in this sort
of employment. As soon as the men hear that the job is finishing
up, they lose all interest in it and it's only with a great deal of
reluctance that they turn up at all. They're only waiting for the
day on which they'll leave to come and it's impossible to get
any work out of them.

Big Bartley was as charmed as a child that his exile in Stanford in the Vale was approaching its end and he began to paint
for us the delights of the city.

'I'll be in the *Shamrock* on Sunday night next and I'll be
plastered,' he said, 'Round there by the Elephant, we'll have
the good time and won't it be wonderful after this deadly camp.
I'll never set foot inside a camp again as long as I live.'

The Leenane men were in no laughing mood and it's no
wonder for they were doing well out here saving a stack of
money.

* Where both Irish and English are everyday languages.
† Where only English is spoken.

Tonight, Corky put on his new suit, his shirt and his hat to see how they looked and I must say that he was a fine sight of a man when he was properly dressed. I thought that he'd get melancholy when he was dressed like this and that he'd be off to the pub but, mind you, no. He took off his clothes again and moved up to the stool where he held forth about the terrible things that had happened in Kerry during the Civil War.*

Big Mouth Grimsby couldn't let him away with it but started to give his own reasons why that dreadful war started. I'll say this for him—he understands Irish history more than most of the English; but he has a rough cacophonous voice that would remind you of the braying of a donkey and you'd have no desire to listen to him at all. From there, the talk moved to the border and Partition and the story of the Treaty was fully debated; every man had his own opinion, none of them knowing the facts of the tragedy if only the truth were told. Little Geordie was doing his best to follow the story, but the more he tried to understand the story, the more bewildered he got.

'Let's get it straight, now,' he said, his brow furrowed as he tried to encompass the sinuosities of Irish politics, 'there's Orangemen and Nationalists and Unionists and the A.O.H. Well, then, who's this other crowd they call the Culchies?†'

Everybody exploded with laughter. But, indeed, it's not the first time that an Englishman has been bewildered by developments in Ireland.

One of the lads came in from the village and told us there was a real rough-house down in the pub between the Connemara men and the Dublin men. Big Bartley and Tom were there, so we heard, and it seems that an ugly battle took place. They're lucky not to have to spend Christmas in prison. In a way, I suppose, it must be a terrible scourge for a little place like this to have so many wild people on their door-step. The pubs, and some of the other shopkeepers also, do well out of the strangers but so far as the rest of the inhabitants are concerned, they couldn't have much of a welcome for many of our boys. I can see 'Arry or George when he gets home to his wife tonight: 'Har, Oi see the Oirish boys be a-killing and a-smashing one

---

* 1922–23.
† A contemptuous term for countryman.

another again tonight outside the *Red Lion*. Wonder why they don't send them all back to the Emerald Isle and let them have a right old do.'

Down on my two knees I was, trying to say a few prayers when that little frightened Englishman called to me. I raised up my head to find out what he wanted and he says: 'Say one that none of them Dublin Pateens gets a bed in this hut, matey, or we shall have had our lot.'

I nearly puked again this morning with the stink of the fish in the canteen. Why the hell they have it at all, I don't know, seeing that they can't get it fresh. And it's not even as if the weather is too warm. It's just as well that we have permission to eat meat on Fridays or we'd be in a right fix.

I met Keady from Spiddal in the canteen at Brize Norton and we had a right good chat. Some Kilkenny chap was with him, from Three Castles and he got a great shock when I started asking him about a lot of people from that area. He had learned a fair amount of Irish from Keady but I wasn't surprised at that seeing how the people of Three Castles had always loved the language. I recall Brigid Clohessy from that place; you would think that she had been reared in the Ring Gaeltacht,* her Irish was so good and fluent. Johnny Lanigan was good, too, and there was a school-teacher out there that never spoke a word of English to his family at all.

I must say this much about the Kilkenny people: even if they are in the middle of the Galltacht, there are no people that have so much regard for Irish as they have, and it comes from their hearts when they say to you that you are a 'fluent Irish speaker'. Isn't there a great difference now between their attitude and that of the bulk of the people in the City of Galway? The Gaeltacht is almost on the threshold there and Irish is spoken widely even in their midst but they have no regard at all for it and they'd live forever jeering at an Aranman or a Connemara man. I'll tell you the difference between their two outlooks: In Kilkenny, they think that Irish speakers are a bit better than anyone else; in Galway, they think they're a bit lower than other people.

* The Irish-speaking district at Ring, Co. Waterford.

Because there was nothing to do, I found today very long. There was a little bit to be done all right but nobody bothered about it. They strolled around just to pass the time and paid no attention whatsoever to the foreman. It's easy to see that it's not Pat the Tailor that they have here for he wouldn't stand for this kind of activity at all. But I'm thinking that I'd be quicker to do something for Tom Keady who would be decent to you than for someone who would be 'coming the dog' on you in order to get something done. I was sorry that I hadn't a book of some kind that I could read in some old hole and that would pass the day for me a bit more quickly.

I dreamed again last night that I was in a little sweet shop all by myself. The woman of the shop had gone off and I had the whole place to myself. With nobody there to see me, I had the temptation to pinch a fistful of sweets. I stood there between two minds and somehow, the sense of temptation is sweet beyond all bounds. Now and again, I yield to my baser feeling and as soon as I do, the desire for sweets disappears altogether and I no longer have any interest in robbery. Until recently, I thought that I was a robber by nature but now I think that there's some deeper reason for the whole thing. What I seem to be about to steal, I have really no wish for. I think that what I want to do is something that is not permitted—and just because it is not permitted. Sin for the sake of sin, you might say. Whatever about that, I understand from the dream that the sweetness comes from refusal of, and not from yielding to, temptation.

Coming from Mass, I had a chat with a very nice man. He came from Limerick and he has a wife and family back home. He receives Holy Communion every Sunday and he is a member of the famous Confraternity in Limerick. There are plenty of the lads here that never attend Mass at all but lie around on Sundays playing cards or reading the papers.

It's terrible how irreligious this country is, for it has many qualities that are closer to Christian values than much at home in Ireland. Take the Welfare State, for example. An awful lot is both written and spoken back in Ireland about this system. But in this country it's not bringing Communism any nearer and it never will. The average Englishman has a deeply-rooted opposition to any dictatorship whatsoever—communism, fascism, or the kind of thing you get in Spain or Portugal; and my own opinion is that, although we are Catholics, we would accept a dictatorship quicker provided only that it came from within our own country.

My own belief is that there is nothing but good in the English Health Service. Go into any doctor here. You find yourself in a nice warm room awaiting your turn. When you get in to the doctor, he greets you pleasantly even though he may be busy enough. He'll give you to understand that you are a person and not a beggar; and he'll give you a prescription to take to the chemist where the best drugs and medicines are given to you with a heart and a half.

At home, such as I saw of it, if you get a ticket to go to the doctor, you have to wait in an old ruin of a house. Look around you and all you see is poverty, despair and dirt both on people themselves and on their clothes. The people go in to the doctor as they used to go in to the aristocrats or the landlords long ago—shaking with humility.

I remember waiting in Kilkenny dispensary one time. The place was full of old women whispering together as if they were going to Confession instead of going to see a doctor. After a while some gentlewoman came in and without taking any account of the queue of people went straight in to the private apartment of the doctor. She spent about an hour there and as she had a hard loud sharp voice, the rest of us were left in no doubt at all about what they were talking about—golf!

This is my last night in the camp. I suddenly got a lonely enough feeling as I thought that I mightn't be able to come back here after Christmas. The Canadian chap was playing the mouth organ in a mournful and slow fashion and that added to my own gloom in some way. Corky is getting very happy as the time draws near for him to go home and I'm not sure that he is not a bit doubtful as to how he'll fare after all these long years.

*Monday, 22.12.1952.* I got up at the usual time and after breakfast I got a lift into Farringdon on a Higgs & Hill bus. I took the bus from Farringdon to Swindon, was delayed a bit there and then another bus on to Bristol. We had a bit of a wait in Chippenham and I noticed the short narrow streets and the low hills in the place. Down we came through Gloucestershire then and I was thinking how lovely it must look in summertime. It is a beautiful comfortable countryside that never knew the hardship and the pain that many of its own sons wreaked on our poor Ireland.

We had a long wait in Bristol and I went around at my leisure looking at the place. A lot of bomb damage occurred here during the war but they're building it up again. I had a couple of drinks here and there but I didn't see any Irishmen although they're supposed to be plentiful enough here. Some of the back streets are very squalid but, then, that's hardly any cause for wonder seeing that Bristol is a very old city.

In the afternoon, I took a train from Templemead station to Fishguard. My father was on this very same station in 1915 on his way to France with thousands of others that had enlisted in the 'Munsters' to fight for the freedom of 'small nations'. He came home five years later with more sense and fought for the freedom of another small nation—Ireland. Two old women were with me most of the way into Fishguard and although I got fed up with their company, I couldn't ignore their pleasant matronly ways. At any rate, they seemed nearer to a couple of countrywomen in Ireland than they did to a couple of English countrywomen—we were of course only a short distance out of Wales.

I got a berth easily enough on the boat, the *Great Western*, and I went to sleep as soon as it started drawing away from the quay. There was a good crowd aboard and I noticed this much —that the men going home by this route were not nearly as big or as handsome as those you see going by Holyhead. Maybe the reason for this is that these people are all city people while the others are country people. I slept reasonably well although the boat was rolling and the waves beating against its sides. There was one small group that didn't stop singing all night and nice enough they were at that.

I got up as soon as day broke and I washed and shaved myself before going up on deck. As the dark cleared away, we began to

66

get a lovely view of the country on every side of us. Two men were fishing from a curragh beneath us, their lamps still burning. Some people started calling them and they waved in our direction. Then some man started up 'The Lark in the Morning' on his tin whistle and I could feel the heart rising within me.

Next thing was we were looking at Waterford City and the old-fashioned houses and stores looked beautiful under the morning light. They were very slow clearing us through the Customs and by the time I got by, both the bus and the train that would have taken me to Kilkenny had gone. It's a damned bad arrangement, not to be able to get out of Waterford until the afternoon but I had no intention of waiting until then. I had a nice breakfast in a little café and headed out along the road to Kilkenny on my own two feet.

At the top of the hill just where the Dublin road and the Limerick road meet at a junction, I looked down on the City and the rocks along by the water. It was a great sight, to be sure, and I felt light-hearted as a little lark. But I couldn't spend the whole day gazing away at the countryside for I had a long way to cover. I got my case up on my shoulder and started to slog away again.

I had got as far as Dunkitt before any motor stopped for me. In the *Come On Inn* at Dunkitt I had a jar—a pint of Guinness—and how good it was. The publican came from Donegal and he told me that he had spent twelve years working in a pub on the Edgeware Road in London.

I had hardly left the pub to move along another bit of the road when a car pulled up and I was told to get on in to it. It was a farmer and he took me along as far as Mullinavat. A nice talkative man he was, God bless him, and he questioned me closely about life across the way. He didn't think much of England, however, and he said Ireland was a better country any day of the week. I didn't want to start an argument with him but I felt like telling him that he'd change his tune if he had to leave his home the next morning and go over to look for work.

He dropped me at Mullinavat and I moved off to look for a bite to eat because the drink and the walking had made me very hungry. I went into this house anyway and the woman

67

of the house told me to leave my bag down and move up to the fire while she was preparing the bit for me. Well, we started chatting away and, in due time, she asked me where I came from. When I told her that I now lived in Kilkenny but that I was born and reared in Galway, she evinced more interest in me and I gathered that she herself was from Roscommon. I discovered that she was a daughter of a very nice woman, Mrs. Quinn, who used to come on holiday long ago to Salthill. I had worked for a while in the hotel where her mother had stayed and we had been friendly.

Well, when she found out who I was, she gave me a great welcome just as if I had come down from Heaven itself. She called her husband and introduced us. When I had eaten, she wouldn't take a penny from me and her husband took me out to the pub where we started knocking back a few of the big bottles they use in this part of the country. Neither of us felt the day passing and I only just managed to get the bus to Kilkenny that evening. The bus was moving away when the Roscommon woman dashed out and hailed the driver. Only for that I'd have been left behind. The fuss there was getting us out of the pub, the boys urging us on, the woman of the house stuffing my bag into my hand and the man of the house, like myself, half-seas over. I managed to throw some money to the boys before I was thrown into the bus myself; and so I went on my way.

There were two oul' wans behind me in the bus and I was fed up to the back teeth with them long before we came to the end of the journey. This is the sort of chat they were going on with: 'Well, then, Phil Walsh's family are doing wonderful for themselves surely. There's John, now, he's a solicitor up in Dublin and Martin has gone for the priesthood. Jimmy's in the Fisheries Department and doing very well too, I'm told, and Nancy married to a chemist in Waterford. Everyone of them doing well.'

The other oul' wan was just as bad; there was nobody she knew that hadn't got a nice soft big job. 'You're at home all right, Danny, my boy,' I said to myself with some bitterness. Fair play to Connemara, that's not the sort of talk you'd hear going back on a bus but gay lively conversation instead. Well enough have we adopted English habits at a time when the English themselves have left them all far behind.

As soon as we reached Kilkenny, I made no delay whatsoever but went straight away up home. The big Christmas candle was lighting in the window and there at the door was the old lady herself to welcome me. Into the kitchen I went and there was a huge fire there and the old man himself was delighted to see how well I was looking. Brian and Dympna came in shortly afterwards and I gave them the presents I had brought along with me. When I sat down to table, I had a huge feed and the cleanliness of the house was in itself the best sauce I could have had with the food. The holly was already up with its little red berries showing plentifully and out in the scullery there hung an enormous goose ready to be cooked.

The old man and I got up after a bit and moved off down to Larry's place where we had a nice cosy drink among all the old neighbours.

# 4

# Back in Northampton

---•••---

On New Year's morning, I reached Euston after a good journey. I slept indeed the whole way from Holyhead. A nice little girl from Ballyconlan in County Mayo sat beside me the whole way down and I think she slept as much as I did myself. London she was heading for and for the first time at that; I hope she does well there for she was a decent kindly girl. In fact I'd like to meet her again but I don't suppose that will ever happen. For myself, I didn't delay at all on reaching London but took a train straight from Paddington out to Callow about two miles from the Higgs & Hill camp at Stanford in the Vale.

I walked to the camp and asked for work as soon as I got there. They had no work for anybody there, I was told, but if I went up to London and enquired at the head office, they might find me something. If I'm sent out on a job from that office, I'll get two guineas subsistence as well as the weekly pay packet; so I'll get there tomorrow and see what happens.

I slept that night in one of the empty beds in our old hut. I couldn't draw my bedclothes from the store since I wasn't employed on the site by anybody but the lads gave me a blanket apiece and I slept well enough. Most of the lads haven't yet got back from holidays and the room looked very bare and lonely somehow. There's no sign of Corky so far, wherever he is. He's a ganger and if he only got back he'd be able to give me a start of some kind.

Instead of going into London, however, I went down to Farringdon on one of Ronan's lorries: he was a sub-contractor like Red Pete and I hoped to get a job from him. Ronan came from Ballycallan and I knew that if I could see him, I'd have no trouble getting a start. However, I ran into a big bad-tempered ganger who only grunted that there was no work for anyone there. I was sorry then that I hadn't gone on up to London to Higgs & Hill.

So I made my way back to the camp then and spent the day in the hut reading. I've no right to be here at all now seeing that I've no work on the site; and the authorities don't like people hanging around who have no business in the place. I'll get along to London in the morning, with the help of God, and if there's nothing doing there, I'll get along back to Northampton for the money is getting short and I can't make out without work of some kind. Fine and comfortable I was here before Christmas with a good job and every right to be in this camp. It's a pity I didn't ditch Lowery before Christmas and get a job from Higgs & Hill. It was easy enough to get taken on then but the frost is thick on the ground just now and, likely enough, there'll be nothing doing here until this month is over.

I kept a good fire in throughout the day and when the lads came back from work in the evening there was plenty of heat in the hut for them. Somehow, I don't get the same old satisfaction from this place now and I don't feel at all that I'm one of the boys.

What do you think but we heard tonight that Corky never went home at all but stayed around Paddington until he drank everything he had! I pitied the poor devil when I heard this story particularly as he had been talking about it so much. There must be some deep reason why the poor fellow is so reluctant to go along home at some stage.

I got up early and caught the 8.8 a.m. from Callow for London. I didn't bring my bag with me for I was really hopeful of getting a job from Higgs & Hill but I'm sorry to say that I didn't succeed. The clerk told me that they wouldn't be sending anyone out the country for a while yet. I moved over to Acton, then, to Lowery's office, to see what was going there. His big Scots secretary was in the room but he told me that there was nothing doing just now.

I was on the point of leaving when in came Peteen himself. He greeted me in Irish and I mentioned that I was looking for work. The Scot didn't know from God what we were talking about and I'm damn sure he wasn't a bit pleased. In the end, Lowery told me to go out to Raynes Park tonight where they would be pulling cables.

I was satisfied enough in myself then having got some work so I went over to the Elephant and Castle to see if there were any Connemara people there that I'd know. I could have made the journey down to Stanford in the Vale to get my things but I was fed up with travelling and I said to myself that I'd be sure to get some old pair of trousers out there to pull over what I had on.

I ran across Big Bartley in the pub beside the *Shamrock* (a dance hall belonging to Caseys the wrestlers) and he told me that he was himself on the job out at Raynes Park. He didn't intend to go out there tonight because it was a long stint from half-past eleven tonight to four o'clock tomorrow afternoon and they had to work very hard. I said I'd pass it up this time too for I was feeling a bit tired with all the travelling I had done in the last two days since I left home. I'd start on Monday morning.

Who do you think I saw then but the 'pincher' to whom I had given the half-sovereign in Northampton last year; but if he saw me, he certainly didn't pretend. Haven't they little thanks, these beggars? I then went over to the dance in the *Shamrock* and met plenty there. They're all Connemara people that come here and it would go hard with you to find a word of English there. Joe Green (Joe Paddy Pats) from Mweenish was there, his sister Maggie and Maire Molloy from Ardmore as well. As well as them, I met Peter Naughton from the same town and we spent some time reminiscing about the old days when we were both in the First Battalion in Galway. Colm was there too and he half-plastered.

72

Carna people are more than kindly and Paddy Pats' relations and Maire Molloy gave me as big a welcome as if I had been one of their own family. I thought ruefully of the days when I was wandering back there to the dances and the decent kindly people that were all around.

I left the dance a bit early as I had to go and find a night's lodging for myself. I made my way down Harrow Road until at last I found a place to stay. I felt like going down to Ward's in Maida Vale but at the same time I was a bit reluctant to do so as his wife Maire had thrown me out the year before for taking Packy out drinking. Up I went to the bedroom that the land-lady offered me. But I found a man in the bed already and damned if I knew what on earth to do. Anyway, he told me to get in beside him which I did as I didn't think I could get any-where else at that time of night.

A bloody big fellow he was and I nearly fell out of the bed as soon as I got into it. Talkative, too, he was and he told me that he had spent most of his life over in Boston. He lost his wife a long time ago and had one daughter. This girl was responsible for his leaving America. She had been bad with asthma ever since she had been born and he had spent years taking her from place to place hoping that the poor creature would improve. He had spent everything he earned doing this; and isn't it strange that, in the end, she didn't get her health until they ended up here in this foggy city. So they've been here ever since—the daughter working in a hospital and the old man out navvying.

After I had got his life story—a Murphy from Cork he was—he started giving out the Rosary and I answered him. I must say that this amazed me for long as I have been in this country this is the first time that I have come across two strangers in the same bed saying the Rosary together.

We got a great breakfast next morning and I must say I liked the company I found below at it. They were all from West Cork and I could hardly understand the half of what they were saying. At first, I thought they were speaking Irish but, indeed, no! Murphy and I went off to Mass together. I was astonished at the sermon that was preached—all about the lads fighting in the pubs and dance halls. The priest came out very strongly

73

against them, saying they were nothing but ignorant beasts that let down their country and their Faith. There's no denying that this sort of thing is necessary for the devil has seized hold of enough Irishmen here in London.

I spent the morning drifting around Petticoat Lane gawking at the market there. The traders here on Sundays are all Jews and I'm telling you the place is well worth seeing. In the summer, the place is full of Yanks and other tourists. But there was nothing much doing there today.

In the afternoon, I went to a nice enough picture, 'Whiskey Galore', and then on to the dance that evening at Old Street. I was hoping to see the Grealleys from Rosmuc there for they had often spoke about the place but they didn't turn up. I met Tom O'Flaherty but nobody else that I knew. I moved off home early enough. Murphy and I stayed talking until very late in the night and again we said the Rosary together.

I made my way out to Raynes Park and, if I'd known what I was doing, I'd never have gone at all. Lowery had only night work to offer whereas I thought I had only to get out there in the morning and start off. Damn it all, I've only myself to blame that I didn't know my business properly to begin with. Anyway, I decided that I might as well go then and get my clothes from the camp. So off I went on the train to Berkshire. When I got to the camp, I thought I was going to be settled for the welfare man said he could get me a job cleaning out the canteen but, damn it, the job had been taken by another lad and I had to go without. Round I turned, hoked my stuff up on my shoulder and made my way back again to London.

There were three Corkmen on the train with me that had been sacked from the job. It's easy enough to get the sack here just now for there's not much doing and they don't like paying men just to be hanging around idle. When the men are doing nothing, they get paid for thirty-two hours and they can live on that together with the two guineas subsistence money. One of the lads was real gas. He'd out-talk a professor and you'd have to laugh at him. He looked out of the window at the animals contentedly chewing away in the fields and said:

'Musha, isn't it well for ye, lyin' out there having yer tea-

74

break and the poor oul' Pats ran outa Stanford in the Vale.
Back into that dirty old smoke now and everyone shunnin' you.
He's no good! Take care would he tap you for a couple of bob.
He's back on the scrounge now so watch out.'

I left my bag up in the lodging and stayed in for dinner there.
The landlady came from Cork originally but she has been in
London since she was a girl so she hasn't a trace of the beautiful
Cork lilt. I went up to bed until it would be time for me to go
out working on the line and I was fed up enough with the whole
thing for the devil himself is better than night work. If I'd only
known, indeed, that wasn't to be my lot at all for when I got
along there none of the gang had arrived and I was told that
the work had been finished since the afternoon and that the
workers had been moved to another place.

And to cap the whole bloody thing, the last train had gone
back to London and there I was left cooling my heels until four
in the morning. I had to spend the night in the waiting-room
and I was fit to be tied lying there in a hard bench trying to get
some sleep. The porter that was on night-duty came in a couple
of times and threw a couple of buckets of coke on the fire. Only
for that, I'd have been frozen stiff by morning.

*Twelfth Day.* This is a Holy Day at home but I didn't even
manage to get to Mass. I've had right bad luck for some time now
and all my money is nearly gone. Unless I get something to do
quickly, I'll be in a right fix. In to London I went on the five
o'clock train and had a bite of breakfast at the station. I met a
gang from the Joyce country (in Galway) at the platform.
They're working for Thady Coyne who is himself from those
parts but as far as I can gather from them everywhere around
London is fairly slack these days.

I went over to Lowery's office to find out where the gang had
moved to but he told me that he had had to let a lot of men go
as there was nothing to do. He said I was to come back in a
week and that maybe something would have started by then;
but it's hardly likely that I'll go. If I don't get something to do
here in the next couple of days I'll go back to Northampton
where I know the ropes a bit better.

I spent the afternoon walking around the West End looking

75

at the shops. I'll say one thing: it's no place for the likes of me
that has little money but it was nice to watch the wealth and
grace as a change from the pinching and scraping of my own
way of life. I've often said it before, looking through restaurant
windows at the mighty ones eating and talking, that it was well
for them that had it easy from the time they were born: the
likes of those you see here in the West End—men and svelte
beautiful women—that have mental and bodily gifts as their
heritage from the ancestors that wrung their wealth out of the
poor. They got the best of everything—the best of schooling,
the best of living, the best of health and nothing to worry them
but where it would be best for them to seek pleasure.

I looked in at a couple of sites on my way home but there was
no work going on—everything had stopped on account of the
frost like most other places. There's no point in going on like
this; I'll go back to Northampton tomorrow.

I moved out of London by midday and reached Northampton
sometime before two o'clock. The first person I met as I got off
the train was Tom Hopkins from Cornamona in Co. Galway
and the story he had to tell me was that my brother went and
enlisted in John Bull's army two days or so before Christmas.
Lack of money made him do it, the poor devil. He had been
three weeks out of work and he hadn't enough upstairs to go
looking for the dole or anything else.

I nearly lost heart altogether then for I had been depending
on Noel to stand by me when I got here. Tom was staying with
Old Mother Dawser, the robber, so up we went to the lodging
to see if she had any place for me. She gave me a huge welcome
but that won't last long when she finds out that she won't get a
penny from me for some time more.

It was an eye-opener for Mike Ned to come in from his day's
work and find me there at the table in front of him. After the
meal, the three of us went off upstairs and spent a good long
time chatting away. Mike Ned mentioned that he was intending
to move off out of Northampton and go working for Lowery in
London but, to tell you the truth, if there was work to be had
from Lowery, Mike Ned wouldn't be only talking of going to see
him. Tom and I started rising him, saying that he couldn't be

got out of this town at the point of a gun and it wasn't long until we had him rightly worked up.

'By God, I tell you Mike Ned has been around more than either of you,' said Mike as he combed his hair. 'I worked at Castle Donnington on the power-house, I worked for Stewart & Lloyd's in Corby, I worked in Coventry and other places—not like you two that bought a ticket in Dun Laoire and came straight to Northampton where you've been afraid to move from ever since. You're not too bad, Donal, for you spent a day or two down in Berkshire; but this other devil hasn't stirred a foot out of the town since he got here—good morrow, Jack! Talk of travel! A snail would do more travelling in a day than either of you would do in a month.'

After that, we had to hold our peace.

For want of any money, I hadn't intended to go out that night but nothing would satisfy the boys but that I should go with them. The three of us moved off down to the *Jolly Smokers* where we had five or six pints of Guinness and mild. We met a gang from Connemara there that had been brought down from London by Pat the Tailor to replace others that were gone. Marcus Curran, Dudley Griffin, Marcus the Tailor and Sean Rua's son were there and a young lad from Kilsala, and if we hadn't a good time together, well, I don't know what a good time is. Marcus Curran has a great voice and he sang two good songs for us: 'Return, O my Darling' and 'The Blackthorn'.

By the end of the night, the spree was great and I hadn't felt so good for many a long day. We left the pub and went across to a café where we had more songs and I don't think the owner, André, would have minded even if we had stayed there till morning. He likes the Irish to frequent his place because they spend more than others and like most of the other Greeks here, André is a thrifty soul.

I felt, as I went asleep, as if a great burden had been lifted from my shoulders.

I got up in the morning with the other lads and went out to Wolverton with Mike Ned hoping that I'd get a job out there with him but it was no good. The foreman said that they weren't taking anyone else on for a while yet. Mike Ned has been here a fortnight and, if he's telling the truth, it's a nice little job. They are making a big sewer and paying good bonuses.

I nearly missed the bus as I left the site and if that had happened I'd have been in a right fix as I hadn't as much as would pay my fare by public transport; I'd have had to walk all the way up to about twenty miles. The driver stopped a while in Wolverton and invited me in for a cup of tea. I had to tell him to go on in himself and that I'd wait for him outside. He must have known from me what was the matter for he took me in and gave me two cups of tea and a fine big sandwich for which I was grateful. Some of the English, in the heel of the hunt, are goodhearted.

Getting back to Northampton, I went to the Labour Exchange to see if they had any job at all to offer. I got a card from them to go down to a foundry in Bridge Street straight away so off I went without delaying. Twenty-five shillings a day they are paying and it's miserable enough recompense for working in such a place.

The first thing I got to do in the foundry was to take a sledge-hammer out into the yard and start breaking up some old iron that was to be smelted. Heaps of this stuff were scattered here and there about the place. I was breaking and smashing away when down comes another man from the 'labour'—Ted English from Achill Island. Ted was put working beside myself and God knows it was great to have another Irishman soldiering away beside me. Neither of us were very good at this class of work. We knew more about shovelling or digging and so we felt the day very long. You can be sure that if things weren't so slack just now, you wouldn't find us here.

We worked away for all that and after a while the pile of broken iron was increasing by leaps and bounds. When dinner-time came, I was nearly perished with the hunger and all I had was a couple of sandwiches of cheese and tomato that I never liked anyway. Ted went off to his lodging where he had a good meal waiting for him; but, if I went back to my oul' bag at that time of day looking for grub, I think she'd probably go cracked altogether. There wasn't a drop of tea to be got in the foundry either, as every man was looking after himself—not like the building sites where a bucket of tea is made to go around everyone. If I was there yet, I don't believe that anyone would ask me to wet my lips. They were a funny crowd, morose and untalkative, and I don't think they had very much welcome for Irishmen. That happens often in works where it's not usual to see Irishmen.

Well, anyway, I couldn't get through the day without a drop of tea so I made my way up to Pat's cafe on the Mayorhold to ask him for a cup of tea 'on the slate'. It's a small poor place that he has but he has never yet refused a man that came to him looking for a meal. I only asked him for a cup of tea but what do you think, didn't he give me a whole plate full of fried bread, two eggs and a slice of bacon. I laid into that grub willingly, I can tell you, and when I pushed the crockery back across the counter to him, didn't he slide a half-crown into my fist! I need hardly say that I'm more than grateful to the decent man particularly as he doesn't do all that well out of the place.

The afternoon passed over nicely enough with Ted and myself chatting and reminiscing away together. Ted has plenty of Irish like many more from Achill but it's not all that accurate. Of course, he's been in this country since he was a grown boy and it's likely enough that his people spoke English to him while he was growing up. He has lots of good stories, for all that, about the migratory workers that used to come over from Connaught for the harvesting and about the simple people that were there in those days. This is how Ted would go about telling a story:

'One old woman from our parts came over to Scotland with the squad for the potato picking. You know what the "squad" is, Mac? Yes, yes, you have it! They were working out in this huge field, anyhow—you want to see the tatie fields up there, Mac—and she was getting very tired, the creature. Old, you see, Mac; couldn't keep up with the youth. Well, the sun was shining down on them and the old lady was wishing that the day was done. She looked up at the sun in the end and says she: "O sun without pity, were you never on hire yourself?" '

Ted would laugh so much at this story that you'd have to laugh with him. 'English the Irishman,' as he calls himself, is well known around these parts, I'd say.

I went to the pictures with Mike Ned, Tom Hopkins and his cousin, Corcoran. We raided the pantry when we got back but there was hardly anything there except dry bread. This is a hungry house right enough.

I was never so unwilling to get along to work as I was the next morning getting down to that damned foundry. And to make the whole damned thing worse, I was put working indoors, hauling huge casks of molten iron around and pouring them into the moulds. On overhead rails, there are wheels that carry the casks (or skips, as they are called) around with the skips hanging by chains from the wheels. For myself, I was terrified in case some of the red-hot metal would spill over on me but the crowd here are so used to it that they can do what they like with the skips without any danger of roasting themselves alive. The air was thick with smoke and smuts and I would have given anything to have been able to get out of the hell-hole into the fresh air.

I caught a few glimpses of the furnaces that melt the iron and it filled me with terror just to look at them. Had there been the screeching and wailing of the souls of the damned, it would have been Hell itself. For the life of me, I can't understand how a man can spend his days in such places when there is work to be had out under the health-giving blue sky. But, of course, habit is what does it. If you were born and brought up in a hole like a rabbit, you'd never know that there was any life other than the darkness and the crampedness.

I spent the other half of the day outside with Ted English and I found it a great relief after my spell with the molten stuff. Ted was feeling very satisfied with himself for he had got another job starting on Monday and he had told the foreman to have his cards ready for him that evening as well as his two days' pay. I was a bit in the dumps because he was leaving while I myself had no idea when I would get out of the place. He told me a lot of yarns and, fed up as I was, I could only laugh at them all.

One of the stories he told was about three dogs that found a big dish of butter one day. They argued as to which of them should have it but couldn't come to any satisfactory agreement.

Finally, it was agreed that the oldest dog among them would have it. Each of them, then, had to tell his age. Well, the first dog spoke and mentioned some tremendous age. The second dog, if it was true for him, was as old as the Old Hag of Beare.* The third dog wasn't quite sure what he ought to say but it so happened that the other two dogs were very small whereas he was a very big dog indeed. So he said: 'I was born old and I don't know my age but damn the bit of that dish either of you two are going to get.'

Ted burst out laughing as he told the story and said 'you might even say that he came the hound, Mac!' He was delighted with himself. And a fine lad he is, right enough.

I never saw the likes of this lodging for hardship and hunger and I've seen a good few. It's getting worse, too. The dinner wasn't too bad once even if the other meals were awful but now the dinner itself is dreadful. I'll be in some other house by next week or I'll know the reason why. The lodgers here are all too easy-going with her and I'm certain that if she laid a plate of grass down in front of Mike Ned, he wouldn't say boo to her. I've heard that the Connemara boys have good digs down in Royal Terrace and I'll give them a chance as soon as I have a bit of money.

We knocked off at twelve on Saturday and I can tell you I felt well-satisfied when we did so. I spent the morning inside the foundry going around with the skip and I was getting right used to it. It's a miserable life these foundry-workers have compared with navvies, as I well know myself. The navvy spends his time out in the open air and he doesn't stay too long in the one place. One time he's out working in the country while another he's in the big town. Wherever he is, there's a variety of people and things to be seen by him throughout the day whereas in the foundry or the factory, a man only sees the same crowd, day in and day out all the year round, and you'd know it by looking at him. He leads a very constricted life and I don't hanker after it at all.

I borrowed a quid from Mike Ned and went out with himself and Tom. We had a nice few drops between the *Cross Keys* and

* An old hag of Irish legend.

the *Jolly Smokers*. I never saw as many 'pinchers' in one pub as there was in the *Jolly Smokers* tonight. I heard that it was a big new job that McAlpine was starting that brought them to Northampton. They looked pretty grimy, the lot of them—old 'donkeys' up to their ears, old moleskin breeches and rubber boots. One of them was from Connemara, Darkie Larkin, they call him and he had a great store of yarns. I could sit for ever listening to him.

The *Smokers* is a pub frequented by dealers in 'scrap', tramps of one kind or another from didicoys (English tinkers), to Irish workers and ordinary navvies. It is on Mayorhold Square, a very old, very poor quarter; and the Kip, the free night-lodging, is on one side with a big ironmonger's yard on the other side. It was a very rough area until quite recently and even now the police have to go down there from time to time to stop the fighting.

Before Christmas, there was a big fight here between Connolly of Galway and Big Darcy of Donegal—out in front of the *Smokers* in the driven snow with nothing on the pair of them but a pair of pants and a torn shirt. It is told that they fought like two champions for a half an hour and that when they got tired fighting they moved back into the pub and started drinking together again.

Pat's Café is across the square from the *Jolly Smokers*: another miserable little joint and, God save us all, if you only saw the company that goes in there on Saturday when the market is on. The like of it hasn't been seen since Ali Baba and his Forty Thieves were round and about. In town they say that once a person starts frequenting this place (the Mayorhold and the houses round it) that he'll come to no good; but for all that, you'd want to go down there for it's there you get the raciest conversation to be heard even though it's mostly from dead-beats and scroungers.

For all that, you come across the odd decent person there such as old Punch Flanagan from Roscommon. He's one of the real old stock—more than decent and gracious. He's very old now and I got a fright when I first learned how long he has been over here. I asked him one night how long he had been in England. 'I came over here in 1899,' he said. I could hardly believe my ears at first. He was only fifteen then and to listen to him now you'd never know that he had left home at all. What matter but you have fellows coming over here and they are only a couple of days in the country and they have an English accent. Ward was right in the First Battalion long ago when he remarked: 'There's no gob like an Irish gob.'

We had a nice tasty breakfast next morning and it's only fault was that it was so small. I could have eaten seven times as much but Mother Dawser is as hard as the devil. It galls her to have to cut much of the loaf and you'd think the tea was French wine, it's so scarce. God be with the old camp where you could eat your choice and fill of everything without yes or no from anyone.

Mike Ned, Tom, Corcoran and I went along to the ten o'clock Mass. He's a funny buck, the same Corcoran—times when he hasn't a word to say for himself and, even then, he'll speak in English if he's allowed to. The other two gave out to him this morning on the same topic.

'What devil has got into you that you think we don't speak Irish?' said Tom.

'It won't be long till you're as bad as English Seamus,' said Mike Ned.

'Why do you keep on spouting English when you know quite well that there's no need for it?' I said.

'I've no idea at all, at all,' he said and if we were talking to him yet, we'd have got no other answer.

The dinner was ghastly altogether with herself tight as usual. She wasn't merry either—indeed the reverse—and the husband slipped out of the house as soon as he got the chance. If I was married to the old hag (God protect us all), I'd stand her on her head and leave her there until she got accustomed to the little bit of control. It's clear, however, that the women have the upper hand in this country and that's neither right nor reasonable. I'm not saying that any man should be cruel to his wife, disciplining her at every point, but it's certain that it's very necessary at times!

I spent the afternoon up in my room lying on the bed reading and went down to the dance in the club at night. After the dance, I left a little nice girl from Gweedore home. I tried to speak Irish to her at the outset but I had to turn to English for she couldn't understand me. I thought this odd for I spoke Irish to many from Donegal in this country and they could all understand me or reasonably well anyhow. I'd have made a date with her another night but I hadn't enough money to take her along to the pictures or anywhere else for the matter of that.

I met the Mulligan fellow on my way home and had to spend a half an hour in the cold listening to him guffing about the number of acres of beetroot he had pulled and this and that. It was all right for him with his belly full of whisky and a good supper to boot—he wasn't feeling the cold at all—but I had to stand there like a frozen pole listening to him. They say that its great sport to watch him in a big field of beet—that he's like some kind of an engine working away there. Mulligan and the other lads from County Mayo and East Galway can earn up to thirty pounds a week at this work. It's easy for them, God knows, to have strong fat heads on them.

Isn't it the devil's luck to have to get along into that ugly hellish foundry there tomorrow?

I hated the idea of the place so much the next morning that I couldn't bring myself to go along to it. I went up, then, by Boughton Green, where they are building a water tower, looking for a job. And thank God they wanted a man. I started straight away and thankful I was to be out working in the open again. At first, I was helping the carpenters, carrying the boards along to them but they started on the concrete then and I had to haul the stuff along in a barrow.

We were high enough up—about sixty feet—and I was nervous at first as I had never been so high up before since I took up this work. I got used to it in the end, however, and after a little while, I thought nothing of going out on the hoist hauling my barrow briskly without any fear at all. There are men who spend their lives working on buildings but who wouldn't get out on any hoist even if they got double time for the job. Right enough, though, I wouldn't like to be asked to go up too high.

There's an educated enough bunch on this job and we had great discussion during dinner-time today. One of the most talkative of the men is from Tyrone, a fine strong lump of a man, and it seems he's a member of the Communist Party. Dennis the other chap was named and he takes a great interest in classical music: Bach, Beethoven and the other great masters; and he has over a thousand records at home.

I like this work very well. I got an hour off to go down to the foundry to collect my bit of money and my cards. The foreman wasn't a bit pleased when he heard what I wanted.

'You Irish are all the same,' he said, 'you come here for a day or two and then you're away again. Can't you stick a job for more than a couple of days?'

'Yes, if it's worth sticking,' I said. He didn't like that but off he went to get my money for me. I only got less than fifty shillings and you can be sure that it wasn't a blessing I left on the place when I moved off.

I spent the day working up aloft and I had a great view of the surrounding countryside. There's a little jackeen from Dublin working here and he'd make you feel rightly ashamed. He started off at dinner-time in front of the English about how little work there was in Ireland and about the poverty. I was going to give him a puck in the gob but I knew that if I did, the others would know that he was speaking the truth. I started giving the lie to what he had said, in a joking kind of way as if I didn't care and I was backed up by the Tyroneman even though he couldn't resist having a go or two at the well-off classes over there. In the end, we succeeded in persuading the English our friend was either a liar or a fool.

The Paddies over here are very much against that kind of thing—that anyone should pretend in front of the English that things are not too good in Ireland. Among themselves, they'll agree that they are but they wouldn't let on to any Englishman that it was scarcity of money that brought them over here. To be sure, everyone knows that it's the lack of a livelihood that's responsible for us being here; but it's not at all praiseworthy that a man shouldn't stand up for his own country even though it has no place for him.

On my way home from work, I heard that there was a lodging to be had with the Connemara lads in 10 Royal Terrace and the woman of the house told me to come along any time I liked and that I didn't have to pay her in advance. What I did then was simply to hand over my fifty-bob to Mother Dawser the very minute I had my dinner eaten, throw my clothes together in my bag and get along out. She didn't like to see me leaving for, with the bad reputation she has, she doesn't find it easy to get lodgers now; but I had to look after myself. As for the lads I left, they'll never move, I'd say. She has them too much under her thumb.

When I got down to number ten, there was a big fire going in the room the men used. All the lads were there. I was more than satisfied with the company and the story-telling that was going on. They're great talkers entirely, the people of Connemara. Johnny John, a brother of Peter John that was here last year, has arrived and he's a nice gentle boy. Colin Grealish came with him having failed to get anything worthwhile in London. The frost doesn't stop the laying of pipes since no concrete is used in that work.

There are two old boys in this digs and you'd have to laugh at them. One of them, John Coughlan, is from County Limerick and the other, Paddy O'Connor, is from Kenmare. They both spent all their lives in Ireland and they're not over here very long. Paddy was more than twenty-five years in the Army and he now has a pension. John spent his life working for farmers and he thinks there are great wages going here. He's more than a bit pious and he doesn't let a night go by without visiting the church. The old sweat is not nearly as holy and has a great passion for horror-comics. There's no time that you meet him that he hasn't one in his fist—that or *True Detective*. He was in tonight getting great satisfaction from this horror stuff and he said to John:

'I'm reading a most interesting story here, John, about a vampire bat that used to come in various forms and drain the blood of its victims. Here's the opening lines: 'O you slobberers in blood, you who revel in the gory——'

'Yerra, Paddy boy, isn't it a queer taste you have for reading? I don't know how you indulges in that sort of trash. Wouldn't you think the *Messenger* or the *Lantern* would provide more suitable reading for a man of your age?'

Paddy, it seems, doesn't contradict his old friend at any

stage for he just continued reading the horrors. It's a great pity that I can't convey the flavour of his talk on paper for that was the best thing about it.

This is a much better house than Dawser's and more bread than the lads could possibly eat is put out in front of them. The landlady is a Dublin woman and it seems that she's a decent person; but the best thing about the place is that there's a nice warm sitting-room there and you don't have to go out unless you want to. Many of the men stayed in tonight, not having much money, and we had a great night yarning away together. Curran is a great talker and he has a power of stories. Dara Griffin, or Dudley Griffin as he's called half the time, is good too but half the time you wouldn't know whether he was joking or in earnest. Years ago, when I heard that man's name while I was in the First Battalion, I had the impression that he was a quarrelsome person for the lads always seemed to call him 'Deadly'. So I was expecting to meet a right diabolical person but I'd say now that he's an intelligent understanding chap.

Johnny John told a good one about this lad that went out mowing the hay for this widow. He was cutting away for the length of the day with herself giving no sign that it was coming dinner-time. In the end, as your man was nearly falling out of his standing with hunger, she called him in to give him a meal. A whole plate of turnips is what she set down before him with some slivers of what looked like fly's wings in the middle. Your man started eating and was knocking back the turnips without touching the 'meat' at all. After a while, the widow says: 'What's wrong with you that you're not touching the good beef, or are you afraid that it will start bellowing away in your belly?'

Your man raised his head up from his plate and looked sadly at the widow:

'By God,' he says, 'if it does, it won't be for the want of turnips.'

Tom Hopkins started here this morning and it's well worth having someone like that working with me. Up above we were, repairing and filling holes in the wall of the tower; we weren't very warm at this work but Tom kept the heart going in me with his many wise sayings and his stories about the people back in Cornamona.

G

The little Dublin jackeen was below us on the scaffold and, after a while, he noticed that Tom and I were talking Irish to one another.

'Are yous two speakin' Irish?' he says and wonder in his voice. We said we were. And then:

'Listen, lads,' says our friend, 'there's a couple of foreigners up here jabberin' away in some strange lingo.' Tom was going to jump down on this bucko and rough him up a bit but I persuaded him not to bother about it. It would have been only a waste of time for there's nothing you can do with the likes of him. During dinner-time, Reg Manley christened Tom and myself Chang and Wong but there was no harm in that at all; only fun.

We had to take on the concrete after dinner and with that work we weren't long getting warm.

I had a letter from home today just before I went out to work. All of them back home are well, thank God, and they say that Noel is better off where he is.

Two mornings now, I'm listening to Paddy and John up there in our bedroom and it seems they're up to some capers every morning. Paddy has to get up very early to catch the first train to Rugby where he is working. He has to light the gas ring in the bedroom and prepare his own breakfast as the landlady doesn't get up till long after that. Paddy starts padding around looking for his socks, maybe, or for a match. It's not long then until Johnny wakens up and this conversation takes place between them:

'Yerra, Paddy boy, 'oor making awful noise altogether.'

'Noise. Am I makin' noise, John?'

'You can't believe what noise 'oor makin', Paddy. You'd wake the dead.'

'O dearie me and I can't find a match.'

'Say a prayer to St. Anthony and 'ool find a match.'

Down on his knees Paddy goes then but not with very much enthusiasm. Usually he has the gas turned on by this as he meanders around the room. By the time he finds a match, I'm always terrified that we'll all be blown up with the amount of gas that he has let escape into the room.

I got a five quid sub from the agent. I won't feel it now until
my pockets are full, with God's help. Things have gone against
me for a while but they should start getting better from now on.
We had a great time with Dennis in the hut for a while as we
sheltered from a couple of showers. We started talking about
Beethoven and the other masters and didn't the Dublin jackeen
start needling him, saying that none of that crowd had anything
on Bing Crosby and his like. Dennis nearly choked with rage
and horror as he heard the Great Masters being mentioned in
the same breath as the other crowd.

'Thirty years,' said Dennis, 'thirty years I spent trying to
understand Beethoven. And then it came to me. My God, what
a revelation.' The tears were rolling down his cheeks by this
and it was clear that he meant every word of it.

One of my friends, another carpenter, says that it's always
like that when he starts talking about music.

This afternoon, I stood for a while on the top of the water
tower looking around at the red sky over westwards. Suddenly,
I got homesick for the old place. I thought of Galway and
Lough Corrib as they would be on a summer afternoon and how
nice and fresh it would be in the shadow of the old castle at
Menlo. Salthill on a summer's day came into my mind then and
I felt that I heard all the noises of the children playing on the
strand and the mournful noise of the Connemara bus going by
full of people. It was as if I had gone wandering in my mind,
standing there not taking any notice of anything but remember-
ing times gone. When Tom called me, saying it was time to
pack up, I was as fed up with my life as any man could be.

I went to the film in the Coliseum and it nearly killed me that
I couldn't go out with the lads for a drink afterwards; but I had
to look after the pennies. The cinema was full of boys running
around noisily and playing together until I had to give up any
hope of being able to follow what was going on. The poor
creatures, their bit of fun depends on their parents' pay; and
then they only have a week-end of enjoyment.

It's amazing how neglectful parents are of their families here
in England. Normally, when the children come home from
school, there's nobody there to meet them as both the father

and mother are out at work. The creatures have to get themselves a bit to eat to tide them over until their mother comes home. What matter only that there's no necessity at all for all this work except that people covet unnecessary luxuries like television sets, contemporary furniture and the like—not counting what they leave in the public houses.

Signs on the children as a result, for many of the working-class families have neither manners nor any discipline, running around dirty and uncombed. If it weren't for the good meals they get at school, they'd be undernourished, I believe.

A great defect like this is the ruination of a decent country. What causes it, in my opinion, is that the people aren't used to the affluence they are experiencing and are obsessed with greed and avarice.

I went into the café for a drop of tea on my way home. Going into the house, I heard the lads there in the sitting-room having great sport among themselves after their visit to the pub; but I sloped away upstairs unbeknownst for there's nothing I dislike more than to be with a crowd that are half-seas over while I'm stone cold sober.

Sunday after Mass, I met Stephen O'Toole (Steve Darby) and a fine woman tagging along with him. It amazes me how reserved Steve has got recently compared with what he was like before he met this one. You'd never see him anywhere now. He has a hard job up there in the ball-bearing factory shovelling iron couplings into the furnace to make them harder.

They say that the like of him for this kind of work has never been seen. It appears that few people can stand it for very long but Steve has been there for a good while now, and I don't see that it has done him any harm except that he's got a bit on the thin side, maybe. God be with the nights long ago when the two of us would be leaving Spiddal at two in the morning after the *ceili* to get back to Galway. Times we were lucky and before we knew it we were back in Munneenagisha. I only had a mile to go from there to the barracks at Renmore but Steve had to slog along to Athenry where he was working for a farmer. He'd have to get up very early in the morning to go out to work but it never bothered him. Some of these lads can certainly take it.

Johnny John and Colin Grealish asked me in for a drink
before dinner and there was no use in my trying to make excuses
to avoid it. Into the *Jolly Smokers* we went and there before us we
saw Tom Grealish and Paddy Walsh who had come up from
Sidcup in Kent for the day. We had great gas from then until
closing time. Afterwards we went out to Martin Conroy's place
in Towcester. We spent a lovely easy afternoon there and
Maire made us a fine tea. The Grealish's were there—Tom,
Colin and Patrick; Johnny John, Paddy Walsh and myself. We
had great sport as we waited for the pubs to open. At that time,
we went to the *Bear* and had a few nice drinks until the time
came for us to catch the last bus home.

We got to Northampton before ten and went down to the
Club. There was a great crowd in at the dance but I was afraid
for a while that the old enmity between the lads that were with
me and the Toomeys would start up again. Everything went
fine until the music came to an end and we were all out on the
street again. It was then that one of the Moloneys started
needling Colin Grealish about the fight they had had there last
autumn. I moved over for it was clear that there would be holy
murder unless the whole thing was stopped in time. I was
warning Colin and Tom to have nothing to do with our friend
for maybe Tom would get drawn into it and be arrested if he
started fighting. They would have given in to me but that the
other latchico wouldn't listen to them.

When I couldn't make any headway with the two of them I
went to Tom and explained the situation to him. Tom came
over and started to take his two brothers away and that would
have been the end of it except that Moloney said something
out of the way again. This annoyed Tom very much, I need
hardly say, and he charged after Moloney to try and catch him.
He got away in some fashion and they let him go.

That would have been all right and there would have been
no more to-do about it but that Walsh from Castlebar had to
shove his oar in and he said that there wouldn't be so much talk
about fighting if they had to get into a boxing ring. Bartley the
Tailor and Colm the Tailor came along with us then and
Bartley lost his patience. He chased after Walsh and asked him
was that remark directed against him in any way. Walsh took

to his heels when he saw your man and Tom Grealish hared after him down the street. Bill MacCormack (who has some fame as a boxer) and a group from Limerick City were with him and Walsh of Castlebar ran behind MacCormack hoping that he would be saved that way. Right enough MacCormack stood up to him and said to Tom:

'What do you want to hit this man for? He's doing no harm to anyone.'

Tom said nothing but just drew on poor MacCormack and left him stretched out on the road. The other lads had come along by this and I think they were so annoyed that they would have liked something to start straight away. But none of the crowd there, despite the number, was stupid enough to want to start anything. There was a strong gang from Limerick well enough known as fighters but they did nothing. As the lads moved off, they took MacCormack with them. Walsh from Castlebar was at home by then, I'm thinking.

That's the way these fights start—people coming along and sticking their noses into things that don't concern them. To-morrow, they'll be saying that the Connemara people began the row and no one will believe that they had it forced on them. Paddy O'Brien from Carna and myself remained behind in case there was any more devilment, but there wasn't.

Well, God knows I was worried enough next morning getting up, as I thought of the depredations of last night. I didn't feel like going to work so what I did is to go out to Pitsford where they were constructing a new reservoir. They're only starting on the job, a handful of men assembling the wooden huts that they will use as offices and stores.

I went to speak to a little old weatherbeaten man who was cutting a plug of tobacco as he watched the gang that were preparing the ground for the carpenters and I asked him if they were taking on anybody. I think he took about a half an hour before he answered me. Then he turned his back to me and says: 'We don't want no wan yet a while.' I didn't feel like putting up with this act and I shot back: 'I see you're as thick as the rest of MacAlpine's ganger-men. Is it an X you put down when you sign for the sub?'

He nearly swallowed his dirty old pipe with rage as I left him there. I felt better after that and walked around to see if there was any other foreman on the job that would be more civil than he was. I came across a big red-faced man that I knew immediately was a foreman. I asked him the same question but got a decent answer this time: 'Call again in about a fortnight,' he said and I knew from his voice that he was from the West of England.

Isn't it strange that he could be so civil to me whereas a man from my own country wouldn't even look at me while he was addressing me. It's no wonder that Irish foremen have such bad reputations here when the half of them haven't the manners of a dog.

It was still early in the day so I went along back to work but I didn't make any excuse beyond saying that I had overslept.

It was a bitterly cold day and I was put up on the top of the building hauling steel bars for the steel fixers. We all suffered up there and when dinner-time came we were very thankful.

None of the lads went out tonight and we had a great spree together in the sitting-room. For myself, I had to laugh at Dara Griffin telling about the time way back when he was camping with the First Battalion out at Oranmore. The 'Horse' (Martin O'Flaherty from Rusheenamanagh) and himself were together in the same 'bivvy' and since there were some hundreds of bivvies in the same field, it was hard to find your own when you had a drop taken. The 'Horse' would roll home on pay night and he would try to locate his own place but needless to say he could never find it. Then he would roar at the top of his voice: 'Where is Dara Griffin's place?' I was in the Army at the same time as the 'Horse' and I could easily imagine the way he'd be. Johnny John is intelligent, too, in his own way and when he'd take his pipe out of his mouth to say something you may be sure that it was something worth-while. I doubt if there are talkers like these left anywhere nowadays outside the Gaeltacht. Even the sound of their talk is soothing and musical and if you closed your eyes for a minute you could fancy the smell of burning peat coming from the fire and it wouldn't be hard to persuade yourself that you could hear the donkey roaring down in the garden.

We stayed up late, with every man contributing his share to the chat. Marcus Folan has such a deep voice that it sounds like a foghorn out in the bay and there's no limit to the number of stories he can tell. I like to hear them talking about home for just like the Islandman,* God be with him, we'll never look upon their likes again. Like every place else, Connemara is changing and a new generation will spring up there that won't have the same attributes that the present one has. Maybe the young won't have the same vices; but they won't have the same virtues either. All these characters are like the sailing boat and the spinning wheel, on their way out; the young people get all their opinions and habits from outside.

There is no doubt but that Irish speakers lose some of their innate dignity when they turn to speaking English. And what would kill you altogether is that none of the descendants of these men will ever speak a word of Irish in their lives. For instance, if any of them get married over here (and few of them will be able to afford to go back and settle down there), it's in English their family will be reared, even if they themselves speak the old tongue, as a lot of the Gaeltacht people here do. So all this Irish that could be handed on to another generation is going to waste. Seeing that this is so, it's a miserable Government that won't do their best to keep these people at home.

But I might as well go off to bed and not be annoying myself with these gloomy thoughts. I can't do anything to solve the problem.

* A reference to Tomás Ó Criomhthain who wrote *The Islandman* which was translated by Robin Flower and is available in the Oxford Classics series.

# 5

# Laying Rails

————◆————

*June 1956.* Re-laying tracks on the railroads in the Midlands is the job we're on at the moment—that and riddling ballast on Sundays. Thirty of us altogether are on the job but we're not working directly for the Railway Company but for a private contractor. We're getting paid at the rate of three and ninepence halfpenny an hour and, as we work six days a week (Saturdays are free), we knock back up to fifteen pounds ten, less tax and insurance.

As for the work itself, well, times it was hard and times it was easy. We'd take so many rails to begin with—five hundred yards, say—and lay the new line in place of the old one. On these lines we do all the work by hand—but, on the main lines, engines are used. We work like this: the first gang comes along with their hammers and take out the 'keys' (or the little 'fish-plates' or clamps of wood that keep the rails in place and, while they're at that, another gang is loosening the fish-plates at either end of the rail. When that's done, another gang (about ten or so) come along and lift the rails out of the 'chairs' that rest between them and the sleepers. As the rails are loosened (they are sixty feet long), all the gang, every one of us, have to lift them together. As we get the word from the foreman, we throw the rail into the long wagon that is there to receive it. Then the 'chairs', the fish-plates and the other little things have to be gathered and put into the other wagons. When all that is done, the sleepers are lifted and put in their turn into a special wagon. All that has to be done then is to even out the ground for the re-laying.

As the worn-out stuff is carted away, the new stuff (though sometimes it's part-worn) is brought along and we start to lay the rails again. The sleepers go down first and then the whole gang carry the rails and lay them in their place. Each couple of men has something like a pair of tongs to carry the rails and with the help of crowbars they are laid into the 'chairs'.

I brought Paddy Dollart with me this morning and the foreman started him straight away without any ado. Paddy is only about a month in this country and he has no experience of this work but he's a good strong fellow and he won't be long learning. He was at college at home until recently and then he spent a while teaching until life drove him over here. It's a poor life for the likes of him and I think he'd go off home again if he could. Well, good enough, he was left with me for the day and I showed him as best I could how to handle the shovels and one thing and another. Fair play to him, he didn't resent or object to the work at all.

It's well worth my while having someone like Paddy working with me for there are a number of things that I like to discuss and I can't do that unless there is a reasonably educated man working with me. Most of the lads are only interested in horses and gambling. Paddy has a great grasp of Irish and, bit by bit, we're giving up English as we talk together. He belongs to Sinn Féin and I don't believe that he'll ever get to like this country at all. It's just as well that there are only four Englishmen working on this job for he'd have nothing to do with any of that crowd. Paddy only worries about questions of nationalism and never takes any thought for social questions. To tell the truth, I don't like the company of Englishmen myself but I don't hate them at all.

Part of the day was spent shovelling ballast out of the wagons and I think that is the work that Paddy hated most. But he's doing all right. Two of the other men in this gang are from Kilkenny—or from Callan, I should say, about nine miles from the 'fair City'—Michael MacCarthy and George Bradley.

George is a Protestant and, for this reason, the lads are amazed how Irish he really is. But, indeed, I don't wonder at it at all seeing how many good Irishmen are Protestants.

To give everyone working on this job their due, they're a fine crowd of boys and it's not often you're able to say that. Rogers is the chap I like best apart from Paddy and he keeps my heart up betimes with his jokes. He is always singing the praises of Australia and at times I'm sorely tempted to go out there with him. He christened me 'digger' straight away and he never stops talking about the great life we'd have out there on horseback looking after the sheep and cattle.

'We'll stay right out of the cities,' he says, 'and have a good healthy life out on the prairies like the cowboys had long ago in America.' I don't know how he comes to think that life isn't really as healthy now as it was then.

Coleman from Limerick was listening to all this and it wasn't long before he put his oar in.

'I know where the pair of you will be from now till the day you die,' he says. 'You'll be where you have been for five or six years—in the heart of the English Midlands, digging away with picks and shovels and counting the pennies by candle-light when the rest of the house is asleep.'

This lad won't believe that Rogers and myself aren't rotten with money since we haven't been drinking much from the time we started on this job. Alas, however, it's not true for him, I'm afraid!

Paddy brought a half-dozen copies of the *United Irishman**
with him to work this morning and distributed them among the lads. Cockney Woods got a copy and spent some time reading it. Cockney is a real old navvy and almost every inch of his skin is tattooed with pictures. He has a belly on him like a cow about to calve, save the mark, but he's the sort of man that could work any young fellow off his feet. When he had read enough, he handed the paper back to Paddy and remarked:

'What 'orrible wicked people we are, Pat. Makes one ashamed to be an Englishman. Still, tell you what, Paddy,

* A now defunct extremist Irish paper.

you come down the ol' *Wheatsheaf* tomorrer night when ol'
'Arry's got some brass and we'll have a right ol' shindy and
never mind ol' Churchill and all them blighters.'

The weather is wet enough for this time of the year but we
don't have to work out in the rain unless we have to get a bit
of the line down before nightfall. Just now, we're passing
through Birdingbury in Warwickshire and it takes us an hour
to get there by coach from Northampton.

I usually bring some books with me to read on the bus but I
hardly get time to look at them with Rogers nattering away
about Australia and the fine time we'd have if we went there.
Something is always worrying him and, before he started off
about going overseas, he spent some time beefing about how
good fruit was for you. He gave up eating meat altogether
when someone told him that it did you no good and indeed the
contrary; and the whole time, he never stopped talking about
how good vegetables were as cures for a lot of the ailments that
people were prone to.

He wasn't very pleased with me when I didn't give up eating
meat. He'd bring a big bag of fruit out to the job every morning
—apples, pears and oranges—and, as he didn't want to see me
dying for lack of vitamins, he would press fruit on me as fast as
I could eat it. What matter but the devil is as strong as a horse
and as healthy as a hound though he always thinks that there's
something wrong with him.

Some of the lads jeer him, calling over: 'Do you feel well,
Tom?' Tom usually answers that he feels right enough but
then a doubt creeps into his voice and he asks why they speak
like that. 'Oh! no reason at all,' somebody replies, as if to imply
that they don't want to pursue the point. At this, Tom gets
extremely nervous and before long he moves over to me to ask
me what he looks like. But no matter what I say then, he's
gloomy for the remainder of the day and he persuades himself
that he's a bit off-colour.

I never saw anybody before as worried about himself with
no cause whatever for it unless I'm very much mistaken.

Pay day again—doesn't the week pass very quickly! Fourteen
pounds sixteen shillings I drew and there's nothing wrong with

that, proud and all as we may be at times. I sent nine pounds off home to Ireland as I left work.

The landlady raised the rents on us by five bob without giving us any warning at all beforehand. What harm—I don't begrudge her the three pounds five for its well worth it even though it's mostly bacon we get to eat. The way it is, her husband works in a bacon curer's and gets the stuff cut-price. Rogers is not going to pay the increase, he says. He went out tonight looking for a room for himself and he plans to feed himself for the future. He can eat what he likes then, plenty of fruit and suchlike. I'm thinking, however, that he had been getting worried about eating too much bacon the last while back.

However it is, I like the people in this house well enough even though they're not as soft-hearted as most Poles. Josef, the eldest boy, has been at school now for a while and he's slowly learning English. I pitied the poor little refugee the first day I saw him for he couldn't even say 'good day' to you in English but it wasn't long before he was coming the heavy on the other boys; and now I have noticed that all the Poles have the same sense of self-importance; and it won't be long until he becomes one of the biggest bullies around the place.

We nearly choked the other night as we were drinking our soup. Josef and Victor dashed in, roaring 'bloody Irish, bloody Irish.' Paddy nearly swallowed his spoon and Jock nearly fainted when he saw how upset Paddy was on hearing the words. It was probably from the other boys at school they picked them up for I'm certain that they wouldn't have heard them from either of their parents.

Since these children speak nothing but Polish at present, I'm practically certain that they'll only speak English after a while; for what they'll want to emulate is what their friends do and not what the older people do. There are people from Connemara in Huddersfield who speak Irish only to their children and I've heard it said that there are infants there that never speak a word of English until they start going to school. But I'm willing to bet that after a while they won't be talking Irish at all no more than our friends the Rajczoneks will be talking Polish.

I went out alone tonight and spent a couple of hours in the

park behind the house. There are few places as pleasant as the same park. It's about a mile long and half that in width with plenty of nice trees surrounding it. Tennis, bowls and cricket are played at the top while down below you can see football (both soccer and Gaelic football) and a little bit of hurling. I like going up to where the cricket is going on and throwing myself down on the green grass. Not that I have much love for, or understanding of, the same game but I enjoy watching the teams in their white ducks and I like the slow even unhurried way the players have. I feel that I'm present at something really native—Englishmen playing a truly English game in the heart of England; but when I come down and watch our own lads with the hurling sticks in their grasp, I get sad and my heart sinks. Nobody would be quicker than myself to go to watch a hurling match at home in Kilkenny when two good teams are playing, and there's nobody that would get more pleasure out of the spectacle; but here, I only think of the scattering of the Gael and the poor state they're in.

We lifted an old stretch of line today that hadn't been moved since the days of Gladstone, as far as I could judge—and the dry dust swirled around us each time we lifted a sleeper. Every other sleeper broke in two as we carried it to one side eaten away with dry rot and it wasn't long till our foreheads were as black as the bottom of a pot.

We spent all this shift moving the sleepers; and what crawled out from under one of them but one of the small snakes that are so common in this country—'grass-snakes' as they are called. I flung the sleeper away and let a roar out of me for I'd rather the devil himself than one of them to come near me. Dead or alive, poisonous or not, I have the same hatred of them all. Rogers drew on its head with his shovel and killed it outright. Then before I had time to defend myself, he grabbed the filthy thing and tried to hang it around my neck. I took to my heels down the line with your man in hot pursuit. If Ronnie Delaney* himself was chasing me, however, he wouldn't have caught me for fear made my feet fly. When there was a safe distance between me and the boyo, I stood there with my heart in my

* The famous Irish miler.

mouth. I wouldn't have moved a step back from now until doomsday except that the foreman, Tom Durcan, came along and snatched the thing, flinging it away into the ditch. He bawled Rogers out properly, mind you, and I never would have thought that he would have had that much understanding in his make-up.

The dry powder that rises out of the rotten wood can't be healthy and tonight I feel a bit choked—a desire to cough but not being able to. I got my own back on Rogers later in the day however by telling him that you could get all sorts of diseases from breathing that dry dust. He didn't pay any attention to me at first for he guessed that I was trying to make him nervous; but I kept harping on it and before long he began to feel bad— or he thought he did. By the time we came to go home in the evening, he was nearly at his last gasp.

'You'd think they'd give us something like those smog-masks and not be putting us in danger of our end with that unhealthy dust,' he said. Cockney Woods offered him some snuff at this stage to clear his nostrils and now he's talking about taking snuff from this on.

I wish I was as healthy as he is.

Our free day is on Saturday just like the Jews. It is a queer arrangement all the same to be off on Saturday and working on Sunday. It can't be helped however for what we do on Sunday couldn't be done on Saturday while the trains are running.

This is the day of the week I like best and I always spend it the same way. I go to the public baths where I have a good scrub and then I visit the library. An hour or two goes browsing among the books and I select one or two; then I make my way round to the market and maybe I have a pint or two in the *Rodney* before my dinner. It's interesting how our habits change too. For a long while after I came to this country, I spent more time in the pub than anywhere else and there was little danger that I'd be satisfied with only a drink or two on my day off. Well, they say sense comes with age!

I hadn't much comfort this morning with MacRory—Rogers had told me not to call him by his surname in English any more

—and I trying to lie in for a little extra sleep. He's trying to learn Irish now and I gave him a stack of comics in Irish hoping that they would keep him quiet; but it was useless. The method he has of learning Irish is to learn off by heart a few sentences from *An Gael Og* and then to drag them into the conversation whatever way he can. For instance, the sayings that he has on the tip of his tongue now are: 'Take that, you rogue'; 'You played a trick on me'; and 'I'll teach you a lesson that you won't forget for a long time.'

When he wants to say 'take that, you rogue,' he gives me a bit of a clout; and when he wants to say, 'I'll teach you a lesson,' he half kills me; so that yours truly is suffering a good deal for the sake of the language. But his accent is great for what he's learnt and if he knew it a bit better, you'd think he was from Connemara itself.

I noticed since I came here that there are plenty of Irishmen who have no Irish at all but who have a good accent, however they acquired it. I often noticed while in Kilkenny the number of people who tried to learn Irish diligently and devotedly, but who in the end couldn't get the sounds right. There are many Irishmen here with no interest in Irish at all but even so they'd learn it quicker than the others if they only had the will to. I suppose the reason is that they come from places where the language has only recently died out.

Paddy Dollart was in two minds today whether to go to work or not for he had heard so much about the heavy work we had to do on Sundays that he wasn't sure that he'd be able for it. He came along, however, and we got Mass at half past six in St. John's Church. They have been talking for a long time about having evening Mass for the workers but it hasn't come yet—a scarcity of priests, I suppose. This Mass is mostly attended by nurses and navvies, the nurses nice and neat in their white uniforms and blue cloaks and the navvies with their Sunday overcoats on them, trying to conceal the dried mud on their working clothes. Both groups meet on an equal footing up at the dance in the Irish Club when they are all dressed to kill.

Up to Newbold near Rugby we go this Sunday riddling ballast. Each pair has to do a given stretch of the line, one man shovelling and one man riddling to get the dirt out of the stones. The dust and dirt are thrown aside and the ballast is then put back between the sleepers. The spaces between the sleepers are are called 'beds' and, at the moment, every pair of men has to do two dozen beds a day. We have to dig down two inches under every sleeper and sometimes a man comes along to inspect what we have done to make sure that we're not 'covering up' anything.

It's very heavy work, particularly as there is so much to be done and we are all glad when the day ends. If the railway workers themselves were on the job, they'd only do a third of what we've got through; but we're working for a contractor    d we're getting building rates (about a shilling an hour more than the railway worker gets) so we're expected to get through more work. And, of course, the lads on this job look down on the railway workers.

I'd like to look after Paddy for a bit until he gets used to the work; but Jock and I have been together hitherto on this riddling and I didn't like to tell him to go and get another mate. The luck was with Paddy, however for MacCarthy from Callan went on the job with him and that was a great help. It's tiring enough work to be carting loads of ballast around and, even worse, you keep on getting choked by the dust that rises out of the stones. Jock and myself are so used to one another that we can keep on going without much rest; but if you had a bad mate, or someone that wasn't of one mind with you, it would be sheer slavery.

As we were almost finished this evening, I looked down towards where Paddy was working to see how he was getting along. He was bare to the waist for, like most men who aren't used to labouring jobs, he found his clothes irksome. His brow was as black as night save for a white streak here and there from the sweat that was pouring down him. He had done his share of the work just as good as the best there.

I heard Cockney Woods saying afterwards that he asked Paddy if he'd be out the following Sunday and he said: 'Such a look of 'orror came on 'is face when I arsked 'im, I fink ol' Pat's 'ad a skinful.'

We went along to the dance that night, Paddy Lennon,

Paddy Dollart and myself. There's a lot of fine women coming along there in recent times but as far as conversation goes they're a bit behindhand. The Connemara girls are great talkers not like this crowd that haven't a word to throw to a dog.

Feeling great, thank God.

We have been told that this job would be finishing up Friday next and that no one knew when it would start again. It's a rotten do to let the men go like this a week before Christmas but it seems that this is the time that they go broke on jobs like this and in building. Not that it will make any difference so far as I'm concerned for I'll be moving back home and I'll stay there for a while.

I did well on this job and was careful enough so that I'll have enough to go on for a while, thank God. But I'm sorry for the married men being sacked like that within a day or two of Christmas. There are plenty of them and they haven't anything set aside for such a contingency: no matter how much they earned during the year it was only enough to pay for what they had on hire purchase. I think that if I was married in this country, I'd rather go without the table off which to eat my meals rather than get it that way.

MacRory and I had great fun pulling the leg of Coleman from Limerick, telling him not to be too worried about being knocked off. He's always been at us, calling us misers; but who'd blame us for saving against the rainy day. We talked about the unemployment that would exist after Christmas for a month or two while the frost was thick on the ground and we painted a picture of the long queue that would be seen every day outside the labour exchange.

'Yes, and ye two will be behind in Ireland sittin' on the hob, countin' out the notes: "Didn't we do well now, and to save that much?" ' said Coleman and he fit to be tied. I then began to compose a letter as MacNally used to do, pretending that your man was writing to us begging for money:

'Dear Fellow Workers, I hope you won't mind me writing at a time like this, but as you know from the papers things are pretty bad over here right now. The queue outside the labour exchange gets bigger every day and there will be no work till the weather picks up. I don't mind going without beers or fags myself, but I can't bear to hear the children crying for food; so if you can see your way at all, send on a few bob and I'll not forget your kindness.'

He nearly blew up altogether when he heard that.

'Oh, that'll be the day when Coleman asks McCauley or Rogers for anything. I'd rather fall back on Judas or Pierpoint, so I would.'

MacRory threw me a glance and said:

'What about that job in the toyshop playing Santa for the children?'

'He'd suit the job very well,' I remarked, 'he's getting a bit grey already and it's so long since he's been at the barber that he'd have no call for a wig—all he needs is the false beard.'

'Ah, I don't know all the same; he hasn't really got the kind manner you need for dealing with children. Sure, he'd knock the head off the first child that came to him looking for a present,' said MacRory.

Your man was well worked up by this and, only we called a halt then, I'm certain he'd have asked us out for a fight.

We have only a couple of days left here and, signs on it, the lads are doing little beyond playing cards and slipping down to the pub whenever they can. We have all planned to go to the pub on Friday as soon as it opens and not to do a stroke of work that day. MacRory is to bring his fiddle along and we should have a good day down there.

I like this part of the year in this country as the time approaches for me to go home and already I begin to savour the pleasure there. I have everything ready, my new suit out of Burton's and a lovely new overcoat bought. A good few of the lads will be going back the same night—Paddy O'Brien and his brother Sean (they have a long journey down to Sneem in County Kerry), Weldon of Drogheda and Tom MacRory himself. Paddy Lennon is not doing the journey at all this time for he's hoping to go to America next year and is saving all he can. It would be better for him to go home because when he gets lonely here come Christmas, he'll get scuppered and find himself without a penny left.

We had a bit of a row in the hut today. The pair from Castlebar went over to the pub at half past eleven and didn't come back until after one. They were hardly sitting down having a drop of tea when a quarrel developed and they gave one another a fierce hiding.

The start of the row arose from something a farmer up in Lancashire said last summer: that one of the lads was better pitching hay than the other. They are old enough to have better sense.

We were paid off on the site today but tomorrow we have to be at Northampton station to get a remaining week's pay and our insurance cards. The manager said that he was sorry to be letting us go like that but that he couldn't help it—and, of course, he couldn't.

MacRory and I set up a good feed for ourselves—potatoes, roast beef, with onions and carrots. He had brought two saucepans out on the job with him since he went back on the meat a couple of months ago. It seems that he read somewhere that everybody should eat plenty of meat and soup in the winter; and since then, he hasn't stopped talking about how good meat is as a protection against the weather and against colds. He has had a room of his own this good while and he gets his own meals every night when he arrives home from work. He tried to get me to share it with him at first when he left the digs but I knew I couldn't stand the change of menu every other week as he got tired of what he had been eating.

Nobody did any work again today; some of the men played cards in the hut; others played cockshots, throwing stones at bottles; and the remainder went down to the pub. What harm anyway; we worked hard for them through the whole year and then they didn't think it worthwhile to keep the men on for another week until Christmas was over.

Every man jack of us went down to the pub as soon as it opened. About thirty of us were there altogether, nearly all Irish, and the landlord got a bit frightened. After a couple of pints, we sensed that we weren't very welcome and the lot of us left and went to the next nearest pub.

Fair play to the next landlord, he wasn't blind to the time that was in it. He gave us a great welcome and told we could have the big room to ourselves if we wanted it. We accepted his offer and it wasn't long till MacRory struck up the music and we laid ourselves in on the oil. At first, we bought pints of beer and 'black and tans' but later we went on to the whiskey and from then on the noise and the jollification got louder and louder. Woody's son gave us a couple of lovely songs and, to give him his due, he was very good. Murphy followed him and, leave it to him, he was every bit as good as the other fellow. He's from Cork and, like most others from there, he has plenty of songs. Maybe some of them were too good and too high-class for the company there: *Fair Maid of Perth* and *When I Leave the World Behind* were two that he sang.

Weldon of Drogheda got out on the floor then and danced a jig for us and I followed with a 'Snake Dance'. When they were tired of laughing at that, O'Malley from Roscommon rose and delivered Pearse's oration at the grave of O'Donovan Rossa. He did it well too, but it left me a bit worried for everything had been going along nicely and I didn't want them to start thinking of the persecution of the Irish by the English or the fat would have been in the fire properly. But as it happened, I needn't have worried for none of the Irishmen put a foot out of place while they were in the pub.

We were let stay on there long after closing time and it's seldom that happens in this country. We set up a couple of drinks for a few old warriors who were out in the bar and one of them came over to talk to myself and Paddy Dollart and he told us that he was stationed in Dublin in 1916. I thought Paddy would take a poor view of him so I started to explain that the poor devil couldn't help where he was sent when he was in the army. Luckily, Paddy gets a bit merry when he has a drop taken and he didn't try to take anything out on the old man.

The coach came to collect us at three o'clock and we only had to collect the shovels and the other tools and off we were. That was good and it wasn't until we were half way in to Northampton that the rows started. I doubt if anyone knows who or what started it but inside a couple of minutes they were all belting each other. MacRory and Murphy's son were dug into one another up in front and Tom threw down his fiddle and nearly half-killed your man. Murphy himself then tried to have a go at MacRory but he couldn't get near him for Cockney Woods and MacSweeney from Achill were having it out in the gangway between the seats.

After a while, you wouldn't know who was fighting and who was trying to make peace. The driver stopped the bus and told them that they'd have to get out on the roadway if they wanted to kill themselves. There was about half a foot of snow on the ground at the time and the driver was afraid that the bus would skid if one of the men fighting knocked against him. That cooled them down a bit and one by one they went back to their seats and we reached Northampton without any more trouble.

When we got to the platform to look for our money and our cards, we found another group in before us—the two gangs working for the same contractor over in Wellingborough—and they were well on like ourselves. When we were told to go to the office window to get our cards, the other crowd thought to stop us doing so for they were trying to get holiday pay as well as what was due to them. Holiday pay is not paid, however, in this country until the holiday is over so it was useless for them to be trying to draw it now.

They stayed there for two hours or more and they wouldn't take the money offered them or the cards until they were paid for Christmas Day and Boxing Day first. Unless they were altogether stupid, they must have known that there was no good in that; and the clerk sent for the police. I moved up to the window when I heard my name called by the clerk but Johnny Darby grabbed my coat and pulled me back.

'You're not from Connemara at all if you take a penny away with you out of this place before we get what we are demanding,' he said.

'Look, Johnny,' I said, 'there's no good hoping for that. You know, and I know, that that holiday money is paid according to the number of stamps you have on your card and they're not bringing any extra money down from London to pay this crowd what they're asking. When did you ever see holiday money being paid in this country before the holiday? And it's not as if you were demanding your rights.'

It was no use my talking to him however and after a couple more exchanges, we started fighting. Weldon of Drogheda jumped in to my aid and the lads from Callan also and Johnny had about the same backing. It would have been a right shambles but for the police coming and separating us. Martin Darby came and smoothed it out between Johnny and myself; and God knows I felt ashamed enough to have been fighting with a man who came from the place I had originally come from.

We got our money in the end and went away. There's no luck where too much drinking goes on, in the heel of the hunt.

*Saturday, 22.12.1956.* We reached Dun Laoire at dawn but it took some time before we were let ashore. The O'Briens wanted to get along to Kingsbridge without any delay for they had a long journey still in front of them down to Kerry and Paddy Dollart was in the same hurry home. Tommy Weldon and I decided that we'd make a day of it in Dublin so instead of catching the train to Westland Row, we walked up to Dun Laoire itself where we had a nice tasty breakfast and then a nice Irish pint. We took the bus into Dublin then and spent a great day knocking back pints of lovely porter.

There's a great difference between the pubs here and those over in England. Over there, they're noisy and uncomfortable but here in Ireland they have a nice quiet atmosphere with quiet intelligent men's conversation that's like the musical murmuring of a stream. It was getting dark when I parted from Tommy to catch the train at Kingsbridge; O'Connell Street and the quays looked like fairyland with the beautiful lights strung along them. One of the big shops had its lights arranged like Santa being drawn along in his sledge by the two deer and as the lights lit and dimmed, you'd swear that the deer were actually trotting along.

It took me two hours to get to Kilkenny and the old man was waiting at the station for me. We had a drink in Larry's before going on home and as we neared the house, my mother was standing by the door watching for us. She set out a huge supper in front of me and started questioning me about thousands of things so that I found it hard to get a bite at all. But the poor creature, she found it hard to wait for one of us to come home after being away the whole year.

Well, this is the last thing that'll go into the diary until the holiday is over.

# 6

# On the Jag in London

◆◆◆

*Sunday, 3.3.1957.* We were a little late reaching Euston after travelling from five o'clock yesterday evening. There was a great crowd on the boat coming over and I'd have had a good time but for the character that was with me. What on earth came over me to get tied up with such a head-case? I always said that you were better off on your own but, alas! I didn't follow my own advice when I could have done so. We stayed on deck until the little red lights of Dun Laoire sank out of sight and then we moved down to the bar for a jorum. I met plenty of Connemara men and they weren't long slaking the thirst of myself and your man. He was absolutely amazed to hear us talking Irish, I can tell you. I fancy that he thought no such thing happened outside school hours! It's many a long year since I and my people left the West but, for all that, I get a greater kick out of the Connemara people than out of any other group.

I spent more than ten weeks at home. A hundred and thirty pounds I had in my pocket going home; but there's little of that left now. And what harm? I had a good holiday while it lasted —drinking and reading and staying out late at night at dances and at parties. It's terrible the amount of porter we drank at Stephen's place the night before I left. Well, a hundred farewells to it now for another year when I'll go back again if God leaves me the health.

We got a bite of breakfast near the station and we went off to Mass in Camden Town afterwards. I met so many of my old comrades coming out of the church that I didn't feel in any way downhearted: Michaeleen Connolly, Colin Bartley Colmeen, Peter John and Marcus Joe Barbara. It's amazing how there are as many Irishmen around Camden Town as ever there were.

I hung around until the pubs opened. I found the pint not so good after all those lovely creamy pints of porter at home. It's not for the sake of the drink I went in but in the hope of hearing about some job that might be going. There's nothing much doing here, however, if what the lads say is true; but however bad I'd be on my own, I'm seven times worse while I'm traipsing this character around with me. We had great music at the *Bedford*—fiddles, concertinas and tin whistles—and there was hardly a jig or a reel that they didn't play. Dickie, the bucko with me, was astonished, for he never dreamed that anything like this went on outside Ireland; but he's wrong. This town is, in many ways, more Irish than a lot of the towns at home. More Irish is spoken here and much more Irish music is played here.

We had a great meal at Pano's place when we left the pub and then we moved down to Marble Arch to listen to the speakers there. Needless to say, it would have been far better for us to have gone off and looked for a place to stay but the character with me was to meet a man at six o'clock who was to get us digs. If I had my own way, I wouldn't have been depending on anyone to help me with my own business but as this arrangement had already been made by the character, I didn't like to object to it all that much. God knows I've gone maybe a bit too sour on the poor devil.

There was great gas in the Park as usual—some speakers being quite intelligent but the bulk of them quite gone in the head. There was a good discussion at the Catholic stand—intelligent questions and intelligent answers. Everyone has a right to talk in this place—but what do you think, the character with me wanted to go for some of the speakers for attacking the clergy. It's easy to see that he hasn't been long away from home. You may bet that if he stays long in this country, it's many the time he'll be shook! We spent our time going from stand to

stand until it was time to meet Dickie's friend. We met him at
Paddington as he was coming from work and he got us nice
digs at Highbury in a Catholic hostel at twenty-five bob a week
and with permission to cook our own food down in the base-
ment. We did nothing more then but we made our way across
to Notting Hill where we drank pints of Guinness in the *Hoop*.
The pints were great and we had some good chat among ourselves.

The friend's name is Paddy Lawlor; he is a member of Sinn
Féin, takes a great interest in the Irish language and in a lot
of other matters as well. He was very well worth while particularly as I had had to put up with Dickie since we left home in
Ireland. We saw Jack Doyle in the pub, too. I felt like standing
him a drink so that I could have it to say later but Paddy
insisted that I do no such thing. It's five years since I last saw
Doyle in Maida Vale but he doesn't seem to have changed a
bit. We mooched off down Piccadilly then to look at the
lights, missed the last bus and had to get a taxi back to the
digs.

Tomorrow, we have to start looking for a job.

I had the devil and all of a job trying to waken up your man
this morning. Even when I finally got him out of the bed, he
took about an hour to shave himself. We didn't bother making
any food but went around to the café for a bit to eat for breakfast. This fellow is going round like a sleepwalker; I don't know
on earth what I'm going to do with him. We ran into five or six
from Connemara while we were in the café. They are working
for Murphy up at Highbury Corner, laying cables; and from
what they tell me, work is very scarce in London these times.

'You might pick up a job down below with us,' one of them
said to me, 'but I don't know about your mate.' We went down
anyway but it was no good. Dickie is hoping for a job in the
General Electric Company. He has only just left college. It's a
damn pity he doesn't get it now so that I'd be rid of him. There's
plenty of building going on down in the West End at the
moment but we traipsed around seven sites without doing ourselves any good. A great deal has been postponed because of
the fuel shortage after Suez.

on looks magnificent these days. They say that spring
nowhere as suddenly as it does to London and I'd say
that's true. The yellow daffodils in the window boxes along
Oxford Street are waving in the breeze and the trees in Hyde
Park are sprouting little green buds under the sun. You can see
it in the faces of the people, too, in the women's clothes and in
the zest of the street-traders as they sell their products. North,
east and south we travelled without coming across any work.
If this fellow with me could only look like a working man, we
might stand some chance but, as things are, he's only ruining
me. I don't like to say it to him but I'm certain that no ganger
would ever give him a start. What harm but he's hoping to get
a job in his own line in a week or so.

It's pretty expensive eating out: the sooner we start doing
for ourselves the better. We ran into Paddy Lawlor as he was
coming back from work and went down with him to Mooney's
in the Strand where we had a nice pint. Paddy's job is not all
that good, I'm afraid; he's only working on the railways. Like
Dickie, he got schooling and learning but in the heel of the
hunt, he didn't succeed in getting any kind of a good job.
As far as I can see, it does a person little good to have any
kind of an education these days. Don't I see young lads
from Connemara across here, half of them without any English
at all, earning three pounds a day working for sub-contrac-
tors while the city chaps can't come within a 'God save you' of
that.

The people from the Gaeltacht, however, have a courage and
desire to get on that the city lads haven't got and its coupled
with unusual strength and stamina. Yours truly worked with
scores of young boys from Rosmuc who between them had
covered the whole of England and very profitably too. That's
why, according to me, that it's absolute nonsense for people to
keep saying: 'What good does Irish do you once you leave
Ireland?' What good is English, is my answer, when those who
come over with only English are only half as well off in this
country as those who speak only Irish?

We made sure that we got the underground home (or as far
as Finsbury Park at all events) so that we wouldn't have to pay
for a taxi again.

The same story we had today—plodding around without any result. I wasted more than an hour outside the headquarters of the G.E.C. waiting for this fellow while he was having an interview about the job he was seeking with some big buck inside. Bad luck to the fool, my heart is scalded with him! And all he got for an answer in there was that they'd 'consider' his case. What matter, but I gather from him that they themselves were responsible for his coming over here—they gave him some kind of promise. I'm losing out all the time because of him since I can't leave London to look for work until I see him settled down.

We travelled out as far as Wood Green where a new school was being built but all to no avail. I learned something today that really amazed me: Dickie has plenty of Irish if he could only get a little bit of speaking practice. But he assumes a funny accent, sort of high-falutin, when he speaks it. During the afternoon, I left him for a couple of hours as he wanted to go to Paddy's lodgings up in Paddington and I can tell you it was a great relief to me. I left him at Marble Arch and I strolled pleasantly along Oxford Street to Oxford Circus and then down along Regent Street.

That's a pastime that I'd never get tired of. There's so much to see: all the shops with their goods laid out artistically in front of your eyes; the different kinds of people that pass you every single minute. And where would you leave the women? Undoubtedly, London has the choicest flowers of the beautiful women in the world—or so I think anyhow. Tall, blonde women from the northern countries; black-eyed, black-haired girls from the southern countries; Indian women majestic in their native costumes; and clean-limbed healthy English girls, the excellence of whose upbringing and character can clearly be seen in them. Wouldn't it be a lovely thing, now, to be taking them out to a big posh restaurant for a meal and to be bewitched by their physical beauty and the clarity and wisdom of their intellects. But, of course, this is all nonsense and if I don't get work soon, I'll have other things to worry about besides the wonderful women of the West End.

Dickie and Paddy met me as we had arranged and down we went to *Ward's*, the Irish house in Piccadilly, another place where you can get pints of porter and we had a great night there chatting and colloguing. Paddy Lawlor is a very likeable fellow and like myself, he likes a good discussion. There's nothing wrong with Dickie either, the poor devil, except that he's a bit young for me. He shows a lack of understanding at times also and I caught him a couple of times trying to start a conversation with an Englishman as to who would win the Irish Hurling Championship this year!

Paddy told us tonight that you can usually get work in one of the large hotels. We'll try that tomorrow.

*Ash Wednesday.* We tried the buses today but although they need men badly, they didn't give us a job. I suppose they recognized from me that we were only passing the time until the building work started up again. As for Dickie, I doubt very much whether he'll ever get any work for he has a kind of a 'don't care' attitude about him. The money is getting scarce and we've done ourselves no good so far but from the way he carries on, you'd think we were on holiday. If he could even get any little bit of a job, I'd take the road out of London in a flash. I know the Midlands better and I'd bet that I'd not be long in getting myself some work around Rugby or Northampton.

We went along to try our luck at a hotel and, right enough, we got a job washing dishes. And what do you think of this other fellow who wasn't satisfied with that? Well, I know it's only a low class of a job but I'm going to try it for a while for one.

We spent the evening in the *Hoop* with Paddy. I'm afraid that if we got good jobs in London itself, they wouldn't be much good to us because there are too many opportunities for spending and I'd never save a single penny.

There was a letter from home with five pounds in it waiting for me when I got home later that night. The old lady sent it along to me, may God increase her own store.

I hope to God that I never have to go through such a day again in my life! I never worked so hard as I did down in that disgusting kitchen. At ten in the morning I started off and I didn't get through until ten that night; and as I struggled into my jacket as I was leaving, I knew that it was my last day in that hotel.

When I went along in the morning, I was directed to one of the managers who told me where I would be working that day. He was an ugly-looking man with a pale white face like most of the rest of them there. He had a little cave of an office down below the street level. I told him my story and: 'What, What!' he roared. 'I suppose you're another Irishman come to spend a day or two and upset the duty roster. Can't see why they employ you fellows. Always on the move.'

'Shit on you,' I said in my own mind. He left me with the man who was in charge of the kitchen and then he scurried back to his little hole.

A conveyor kept bringing in huge loads of dishes from the restaurant—knives, spoons and so on: non-stop—and these had to be taken and put in little moving baths, knives with knives, plates with plates and so on. I got a pain in my back after spending a couple of hours at this work and but for the men on either side of me, I wouldn't have stood the day at all. Blacks they were, one from America and one from Africa. The African was a University student and he was working part-time at this job. You'd wait a long time before you'd see a scholar from University College, Galway, scrubbing pots, now, wouldn't you?

We started talking at all events and, when he found out that I was a Catholic, devil another thing would satisfy him but that we should begin singing hymns together straight away. At the top of his voice, he gave forth 'Hail, Glorious Saint Patrick', 'Tantum Ergo' and more, too. I had to give him a hand but, to tell the truth, my heart wasn't in the task. The other man had walked the length and breadth of the United States and was trying to see as much of the world as he could. He preferred America to anywhere else even though the likes of him don't get a fair crack of the whip there.

On the way down to dinner (and a damn bad dinner it was) I met a man from Connemara—a big strong hearty fellow, he was, too. I was amazed to find the likes of him there but, as was the case with ourselves, he had failed to come across anything outside.

'God bless us, brother,' he remarked, 'one day in here is worse than a week shovelling concrete.'

He was in great humour, all the same, and I don't believe that the place affected him as much as it did me. We had just begun to eat our dinner, the pair of us, when a dried-up old French waiter tried to snatch your man's chair. 'Scusi moi,' he said (or so it seemed to me), 'you take my seat'. The Connemara-man let a roar out of him: 'Get away out of that,' he said, 'or I'll twist it around your neck.'

The Frenchman didn't bother us again.

I was set drying knives during the afternoon, a bit nearer to the restaurant itself. I was drying away nice and steady and looking out through the hatch at the girls that were waiting at the tables. I particularly noticed one of them and, by my soul, it occurred to me that she was taking an equal interest in me. A nice slender girl she was, with a lovely fresh face and a shock of black curly hair—just like a girl from the West of Ireland, me boy! I smiled across at her and, what do you think, she came straight across to me. I thought I was well away with it then! As she approached, I saw how really beautiful she was. I couldn't open my mouth. But she was struck the same way:

'Knives,' she said.

'Knives,' said I.

'Yes, knives,' she retorted with every appearance of impatience. 'Can't you see I'm short of knives or what are you dreaming about?'

I was changed back on to the washing then and that's where I spent the rest of the afternoon. I met a boy from Ballyfoyle which is just outside Kilkenny and he had a great wish to talk when he found that I was from those parts. He had been working for a farmer before he came across here three months beforehand and you'd think that he had the best job in England though you'd travel far in any country before finding a more lowly job. Something about six pounds he gets here as well as his meals (God save the mark), and he's more than satisfied with it. 'Be the honey,' he says, 'I wouldn't work for a farmer again for the world.' Well, I've always heard that it's hard to make a choice! When I got out on the street after finishing up, it was like a new lease of life to breathe the fine fresh air after the fug and fetid atmosphere inside. I'll go and get whatever pay is due to me tomorrow.

Dickie finally got news of a job as a barman in a pub at King's Cross and he went along to look for it. I left later in the day and moved across to Marble Arch to look for my pay and my cards. I found the manager down in his little cave and I told him I was checking out straight away. He leaped up, I can tell you:

'What, what, finishing already? I knew it! I knew you weren't the type!'

'Thanks for the compliment,' I answered.

He gave me a note and I had to climb up to the top of the house where the pay out takes place. What I was told there was that I'd have to come back in the afternoon for my money. I laid a heavy curse on them and made my way up to Kilburn hoping that I'd get news of some job. I stayed in *The Bell* until closing time, almost.

As I came out to go for the bus, a snide little fellow was at my heels and he started asking me about how the work was going. He had a brother, he claimed, on a big job that was just beginning and who was looking for a couple of good men. I remarked that they should be easy to find, seeing that so many were unemployed. The bus pulled up just then and in we both got.

'One to Edgeware Road,' I said to the conductor.

'Get mine too,' whispered your man, 'I have no change.'

I was going to tell him to go to hell but I thought that maybe it was true that he had a brother that could give me some work so I paid for his ticket. By the time we reached Edgeware Road, he had promised me the job and invited me to come and have a drink with him in the *Green Man* before they closed.

'Well, by my soul,' I thought to myself, 'it may be that you're not a sponger after all.' So in I went with him. But, alas! as we pushed in through the door, he whispered: 'You get the drinks and I'll square up with you again.'

'Fair enough,' I said to myself, 'I'll play one on you, my little Cork birdie.'

We went up to the counter and I asked him what he was going to have. Stout and mild was what he asked for.

I

'Two stouts and mild,' I called to the man behind the counter,
Then, as the barman started to fill them out, I said to our
friend: 'Hang on there a minute till I visit the Gents.'

I had been in the *Green Man* many times before so I knew the
lay-out of the place well. You can go into the toilet through
one door and out through another. I didn't make even the
slightest delay but walked straight in the one door and out the
other, where I caught a bus immediately. The Corkman could
be waiting for me yet!

But I nearly went cracked when I drew my pay. Thirteen
and fourpence is what I got for my day's work (that was
allowing for the insurance stamp). I whipped back into the
office.

'Sure I got more than that for even two hours work at the
building.'

'Well, you're not at the building now,' the clerk answered
and, indeed, it was true enough for him.

I visited my old friend, Packie Ward, for the first time since
I got back to London. Himself and his wife gave me a great
welcome and it wasn't long until Packie and myself moved out
along to the *Manor House*. There we ran into John Delia and
others from Connemara and, if we hadn't sport that night, well,
we never had it. We passed the whole night talking about the
days when we were all in the First Battalion back in Ireland
and about the great times we had had then.

There is an 'Irish' hall out here so that plenty of Irishmen and
particularly Connemara people come along out these parts.
But these halls are only another racket. The people that own
them call them 'clubs' and there's some pretence about member-
ship but that's only to pull the wool over the eyes of the
authorities. They have rules and aims displayed as if the objec-
tive of the club was to propagate the culture and pastimes of
the Irish. But they're really only dancehalls that most of the
time it's not safe to go into.

Towards the end of the night, a crowd of 'Teddies' came into
the pub and we got a good bit of gas out of watching them
putting money into the juke-box and doing the rock-and-roll.
They were a queer crowd right enough and it would go hard
with you to tell which were men and which were women. 'May

the lovely Son of God look down on the mothers that bore them,' growled Ward, spitting out towards them. They threw us a couple of dirty looks but there was little fear that they'd try anything on with the Connemara people. I think that any country that produces these types must be in a bad way for they're no good either to themselves or to anybody else. What harm but they're not all English. There are as many here from Irish towns that are as much 'Teddies' as any crowd from the East End. It's a class of fever or disease, I suppose, that's not likely to last much longer.

I had as fine a bit of trout as I ever had tonight when I got home. I bought it down in the fish and chip shop at the corner so I'll know where to go for it the next time.

Dickie and I went along out to Edmonton as I had heard that William Moss was working out there and I thought I might have a chance of getting some work from him. Dickie is still waiting for news from the other place but nothing would satisfy him except to come on out with me. The site was as far away as the devil himself but we found it in the end. A big sewage disposal plant is what they're making just where the old one was and it's very dirty work by all accounts. Irish and Jamaicans are working on the job for the most part.

We asked where the office was and we were directed down the field to where an old English 'pelter'* had charge of the navvies. Dickie was jumping from tuft to tuft in an endeavour to keep his shoes clean. When we made along to the old man, I asked if he could give us a start. He bent a shrewd eye on me:

'Are you a good shovelman, Paddy?' he asked.

'Well, I've never had any complaints,' I answered him.

'All right,' he said then, 'start on Monday.'

'What about my mate?' I enquired.

If you only saw the look he threw at poor Dickie: 'What? 'Im? He looks like a ruddy bank clerk, don't 'e?'

I didn't quite like him running down my pal no matter how bad he was.

'Oh, he's a willing enough young chap,' I said.

* A local word for a ganger.

He gave Dickie a rather more civil look: 'Sorry, sonny,' he said, 'we only want experienced men.'

I was half-minded to tell him to keep his job but then I thought it would be good for Dickie to see me working so I held my peace.

The two of us went to the pictures at the Angel that afternoon and for my part I enjoyed it very much. That tune 'Those Falling Leaves' was running through the film from beginning to end and I got a bit lonely thinking of home and poor Stasia. This is Saturday night, and, if I was at home, I'd be having a nice drink down at Stephen's place with a couple of crubeens* to eat on the way home. A week from tomorrow is St. Patrick's Day and, with the help of God, it'll be a good one.

To Mass in Highbury this morning. I didn't find it as satisfying as Camden Town, somehow. It's mostly a married crowd that comes here and you don't find any gatherings outside the church like you do in other places.

We snatched a bit of breakfast in Camden Town at Pano's place and then we stood down at the corner until the pub opened. There's an enormous number of Paddies around this area: from Connemara, from County Mayo and nearly every other county in Ireland. There are a good few from Dublin also, and they're the lowest of the lot. They hardly do any work at all—just sponging around for the most part and shacking up in Rowton House. Any day of the year you can see them there holding up the walls without even a decent stitch of clothes on them and not even the price of a pint in their pockets. What harm but they think they're far more clever than the fine upstanding men who have full pockets—the 'culchies' as they call them derisively.

Into the *Bedford Arms* with us, however, and we stayed there until dinner-time and, by God, it was worth it. The music was terrific altogether. The big room was bulging and I never saw so many fine people gathered together in one place before. We put in the afternoon strolling among the speakers at Hyde Park Corner. There was a huge crowd there and the rhetoric and the joking was superb.

* Pig's trotters.

Patrick Lawlor was outside the Gate selling the *United Irishman* and, a short distance down from him, there were a couple selling the *Irish Democrat*. This is a socialist paper put put out by the Connolly Clubs. Many of the Irish here are against the people responsible for this paper as they are inclined to be very much to the left but I think they're an honest enough bunch who are seriously concerned about the bad state that Ireland is in. It's said that they are Communists but I doubt that. Only a short while ago, I was talking to a priest who told me that the English Communists had failed to get any good out of them at all.

I read something in the same paper once that explains the outlook of some of the Irish here about things of this kind. This boyo was going around the pubs in Camden Town trying to sell the *Democrat* to the lads. He stretched it out to one man who snarled 'Clear off with your oul' paper, the Church don't approve of it.' The *News of the World* was sticking out of the man's pocket at the time. The man with the *Democrat* merely said: 'Just how mixed-up can Irishmen get?'

The other Irish papers can also be got here, particularly the *Kerryman*, the *Connacht Tribune*, the *Anglo-Celt*, the *Cork Examiner* and, a paper in Irish, *Tomorrow*.

Down at the Catholic stand, who do you think I met but my sister who seems to have come over this week and another young girl from County Mayo. She was delighted to see me and I brought them into a café on the Edgeware Road and gave them a meal. Dypmna has got a job as a secretary in one of the biggest stores in London and is getting a man's pay; but isn't it a pity that she couldn't find a job at home with all her learning and skill?

After a while, we went back to the park and we stood listening to the women of the Church Army telling everyone how they got to know God for the first time. They had with them young girls from every walk of life, all to tell their own story. One woman got up on the platform and, like the rest of them, she didn't need any encouragement. Her face was flushed with faith and emotion. She started off in a strong Lancashire accent. 'I found Jesus in a factory,' she cried. Then after what I suppose you'd call a dramatic pause: 'It's hard to find Him in a factory, brothers, it's hard to find Him in a factory.'

Dympna let a screech of laughter out of her and, God forgive me, I was as bad myself. The woman turned on us a look full of sorrow and pity but by then we were making our escape from the place.

We paid a visit to Willie after that. This Willie is a little man full of vindictive Biblical sermons, who hates the Irish and the Catholic Faith. To give him his due, it's hard to blame him for being anti-Irish for it's the Irishmen who tease him all the time —cutting in on him with 'Hail, Glorious Saint Patrick' and 'Faith of Our Fathers', all just to get him right mad. He gets really cross then and clouts the person nearest to him with a Bible. Funny enough, the Irish don't relish it if there's any kind of a disturbance at the Catholic platform.

It's not long ago since there was a good one here at Hyde Park. A Sinn Féin speaker was denouncing England and holding forth about her evil deeds. This annoyed an Englishman who happened to be listening. 'As an Englishman,' he said, 'I should go up and sock you.' Right then, a big constable with a strong Kerry accent, said to the Englishman: 'Move along there now and don't be disrupting a lawful meeting!' The Englishman was fit to be tied!

To bed early tonight.

I had to get up before six to catch the bus down at Finsbury Park at seven. I could only gulp the bare cup of tea before going out. As soon as I got to the job, I was started off digging a trench. It was a gorgeous morning and after a while I felt as light-hearted as a lark.

A young fellow from the Spiddal area was in the trench with me (I recognized him for one of the Currans of Ballinahown) and I gave him a start when I spoke suddenly to him in Irish. We had a great chat after that, gossiping about *ceilis* in Spiddal and the people that came to them. Four and three-halfpence an hour is what they are paying here and no talk of subsistence or a bonus. I'll stick it for a while but that's all.

I was starving with the hunger by the time I got back in the evening so all I did was to change my clothes and go along to Eddie's in Finsbury Park for a meal. There I had lashings of potatoes, as much as I could eat of ham or beef, plenty of cabbage, a glass of milk and a big sweet for three and fourpence and you couldn't beat that anywhere. Eddie comes from Cork and he's always very decent to the boys when they haven't a penny. Mostly, it's Cork and Kerry people that frequent his place and he's given 'tick' to a lot of them. There are plenty of blacks living around Finsbury Park and it's not long ago since one of them came to Eddie looking for credit. Poor Eddie got a fright: 'Oh, dear God, boy, isn't it bad enough to have half Munster owing poor Eddie money without bringing the West Indies into it too?' he said.

There's more Irish being spoken around these parts than in any big town in Ireland. I went up to Stamford Hill to see the Wards and the two of us dropped into the pictures. When I got home, Dickie was there before me. He got the job in the pub at King's Cross and I hope he does well at it.

I took half a loaf and a bottle of milk along with me on the job this morning and it kept me going until evening. The eating place here is a large hut with a tin roof and, as in most of these places that I've seen on building sites in this country, the Irish stick together and don't have much social contact with the English. Most of the workmen read that rag, the *Daily Mirror*. I had brought *Cois Caoláire* with me in my pocket as I left this morning and I read some of it during dinner-hour. Anyone that had any desire to write, he would, on reading Mairtín Ó Cadhain, be between two minds whether to forget about it altogether or to give his whole body and soul over completely to learning his art quarter as well as Ó Cadhain has it.

I felt very relaxed going home this evening, half thinking of staying here in London for a while. I had a good dinner in Eddie's and went down to Piccadilly after that. I could stay walking around there for a long time looking at the bright lights, the rich people and the beautiful women that are always coming and going. It's the bright lights and not so much lack of work that entice the Irish over here away from their own country. 'Good morrow, Jack' as they say! I knocked back two pints slowly and comfortably in *Ward's*. I moved off home early enough.

Dickie will be staying in the pub from now on. He likes the

work well, he tells me. I feel sorry for having been so down on him. Probably, I'll miss him from now on, the poor devil.

We were working away heartily this morning, Curran and myself, when old Bob came along and asked me if I'd mind changing down to the gang working in the field. I said it was all the same to me. But, I'm telling you no lie, if I'd known what lay in store for me there, I wouldn't have been so accommodating. 'Look for Mike Sheehan when you get there,' I was told and off I went.

I found this fellow without any difficulty, bad luck to it. He was a big tough from West Cork and every man working for him is from the same place. 'Oo'll have to put 'oor back into it here, boy,' he roared at me without waiting to see how I was going to shape up. The work here consisted of draining out the old sewer and loading it into skips. These skips run on two small rails and are drawn along by small diesels. They are pulled down to the bottom of the field and the dirt is emptied there. Any time the big 'Navvy' lifted a bucketful of this offensive muck out of the sewer, a good deal of it was spilt on the ground or on anyone who was stupid enough to be standing near.

I was set following the little train, emptying the skips and changing the points on the rails. Barring the dreadful smell, that wouldn't have been too bad if it wasn't for the fact that the wheels of the skips kept coming off the rails every couple of minutes and it was the devil's own job trying to lift them back again. Mike Sheehan would come trotting up with his friends at his heels, cursing and swearing and his two eyes jumping around in his head with anger and impatience. They'd start lifting the yoke and with every movement, more of the foul stuff would pour down on the men's clothes, arms and heads. More cursing would ensue, every man swearing that he wouldn't stay another week dealing with this muck and Mike Sheehan getting madder and madder every minute.

In the end, by the time the bad language had been exhausted, the wheels would be back on the rails and on we could go. Times, we would hardly have moved fifty yards when the skips would go off the rails again and the identical same pantomime would commence all over again. Mike Sheehan would be well worked up by this and it wouldn't be safe to be caught within the reach of his hand. Even the big tough men that are in his gang prefer not to say anything to him on these occasions.

At the end of the journey, I had to up-end the buckets and the muck would pour out in a great big black flood. It took me some time to get used to the points and the first few times I changed them, I sent the train along the wrong line so that it was in grave danger of running into the other train that was loading at the other side of the sewer.

There was one buck named O'Donoghue and he had his coat off while he was shoving the stuff down from where I was dumping it. He worked away without paying attention to anything but growling the while about the smell, the dirt and the pay he was getting. I happened to ask him what time it was and, when he went to look for his jacket to get his watch, wasn't it covered with the muck. I really thought he'd go up altogether, he was so agitated. I signalled to the driver to take me away from the place before your man had a go at me.

Anyway, whatever chance there was up to now that I would have stayed on the job, there's no hope at all now. Tonight, I didn't go out at all.

There were times today when I didn't know whether to laugh or to cry. Despite all our efforts, the train kept coming off the rails at every set of points and Mike Sheehan was like a mad bull, roaring and bellowing away—or as one of the Cockneys that passed by remarked, 'doing his nut.' The Union Pacific had nothing on us as we took the lines apart and put them together again, taking the sleepers out in one place and putting them in in another, while we slipped and fell down in the muck all the time. We got protective clothing from the store but it was useless against the rotting fetidness. To cap it all, the men above said that they wouldn't allow us into the eating-place because of the stench from our clothes and we had to put up a canvas shelter for ourselves beside the sewer.

This gang is the laughing-stock of the whole job and that's the truth. I don't care for I won't be staying here and I don't care about any of the crowd but it upsets Mike Sheehan and his

friends very much. It's like a circus when we get on to the bus
going home in the evenings: one slipping in with his head
hanging as much as to say: 'Don't mind me, the smell doesn't
come from me at all'; another going boldly in with the attitude:
'I dare any of you to say anything, you pack of devils.' But I
must say that I never saw the likes of these men before anywhere
for malice, impatience and vindictiveness towards one another
—even though they're all from the same district. My life on the
Connemara people! They have fun and laughter and great
chat—not like the perpetual grousing that goes on with this
crowd.

This gang, under Mike Sheehan, has been working for Moss
this few years and up to now they were on piece-work so that
there was no limit to what they could earn as they are all fine
strong men. There's no piece-work going now however, so that
it's a big come-down for them to be working on this sewerage
job. I was thinking that there was something like that behind
it all for, where there is perpetual disgruntlement and dis-
satisfaction, you may be sure that lack of money is behind it
all. It's not that they haven't plenty of cause for complaint
working with this muck; but if they were getting well-paid for
it, they'd put up with it cheerfully enough.

This is the second night in succession that I haven't stirred
outside the door. I got a letter from Noel who is in Winchester
telling me that he'd be coming up on Saturday for the Feast
of St. Patrick. Its not far off.

This morning, I told Mike Sheehan that I intended to take
my cards that evening and he wasn't a bit pleased about it.
'God blast it,' he bawled, ''oor not going now that 'oor
trained.' From his attitude, you'd have thought I was an
engineer or suchlike.

If it was my last day there itself, that doesn't mean that it was
any way easy for me, for there were more mishaps today. There
was a little wooden bridge across the stream and it had been
much weakened by the weight of the train passing over it every
couple of minutes. Mike said we'd have to look at it after dinner
or a disastrous de-railing would take place. I was hoping he'd
leave it alone until I was well away from the site but it was no

good. We had to start lifting the rails and putting them on one side. Then we began to strengthen the bridge. We ran some joists across from one side to the other with supporting beams. Both sides of the little stream were dirty and slippery and we had no sooner started than the place became a bog. We were sliding and falling with the water below us and the bridge above and before long every man jack was covered in mud up to his bottom.

Mike Sheehan is the sort of person that has to be in the middle of everything, whatever the work is, and no matter how hard or how dirty it is. On this occasion, he was under the bridge trying to force the head of one of the supports under a joist when he lost his foothold and fell into the stream up to his knees. He was speechless standing there in the water with his two eyes flaming out of his head with rage. Not one of us said anything or moved a muscle but I'm sure that every man was like myself trying to keep back the laughter that was choking in our throats. Then without the slightest provocation, the poor devil bawled at the man who was furthest away from him: 'The Lord may stiffen 'oo anyway, O'Driscoll.'

He took off his wellingtons and wrung the water out of his socks, the whole time calling down all sorts of bad luck on William Moss, on everyone that was working for him and on the people of London for whose welfare this work was being carried out. We had to finish the job without him and, if we did itself, it was done without half the amount of roaring and bad language. Eleven pounds I found in my pay-packet when I was going off; and it wasn't bad for five days.

I called on Packie before seven and we went to the 'dogs' at Harringay. I don't get very much satisfaction from this sport but Ward is the devil for betting. The same races, indeed, left plenty of the Irish without a penny after coming over here. Many's the man goes into Harringay or White City on pay evening and comes out at the end of the night without a penny left in his pocket.

Packie had no luck on the first two races but he started winning then time and again until he was thirty pounds to the good. It was the mercy of God that the last race was over by then or he wouldn't have left the place until he had lost every

penny of what he won. I didn't bet at all. There was a girl
behind us and she was in a terrible spin, shouting and urging
on the dog she had her bet on: 'Come on, you little piggie,
come on, you rat, come on you lovely beast,' until you'd think
she was about to become airborne any minute.

Like every other gambler, Ward is chockful of superstition
and he really believed that it was my presence that made him
so lucky tonight. We went into the *Manor House* where Packie
started off straight away on the whiskey. He wouldn't let me
put my hand in my pocket at all and, indeed, he came the
heavy a bit standing drinks for everyone he recognized as they
came in. After a while, John Delia, Colin Tom and John
Bartley Colmeen came in and we had great crack from then on.

The Teddies, inside where the piano was, were kicking up an
awful row and we looked in to see what devilment they were up
to. The room was big and wide and was packed to the doors
and the band was giving out lustily, 'Crazy man, crazy man, dig
those blues,' or whatever the hell is the name of that damn
tune. Well, this clot was up on the stage, struggling with the
'mike' and, in the middle of it all, he grabs a bottle of milk
from a member of the band and pours it over his own head. A
great cheer went up from the company as the milk dripped
from the chap's head.

'Well, you devil,' said Packie, 'I hope you're seven times
worse off a year from tonight and a year from tomorrow
night.'

'Cor, 'e ain't 'alf being sent,' said a lovely girl standing near
us who was very much taken by the boyo.

'I know where I'd send the latchico,' muttered Ward.

'Why, where would you send him,' said the girl in an un-
friendly way.

'Out to Carraig an Bhalbhain* in the month of March with
a bottle of cold tea,' said Packie.

By God, I thought the look she threw at him would have
withered him up on the spot!

I ate a bit of cod when I got home and it was very nice.

I dropped down to King's Cross to see how Dickie was
_____
* An isolated townland.

getting on. He's well set up in that place if he has the sense to stick it until he gets the job he's really looking for. I saw an advertisement in a shop window saying that men were wanted in such and such a place as waiters, good money and digs as well. I went looking for the place, half-thinking that I'd take the job for a while if it seemed to be any way good at all. But, alas! when I got along, where was it but Rowton House! One look at the big ugly walls and the naked windows and away with me like the hammers of hell! A sour smell of old cabbage drifted up from the kitchen and I said to myself: 'Joe Soap* is not going to wait on them if they were never to get a bite at all.'

Noel and Dympna met me in Baker Street, outside Madame Tussaud's and the three of us went along in to see the wonders. It's a long time since I visited this place but I always get a good deal of pleasure out of it. The Chamber of Horrors is the best part of the whole show and you have to pay an extra fee to get into it. It's a courageous person that would spend a half an hour down there by himself. Each figure is worse than the next: a man with a hook through his belly, another man stretched on the rack, the bones of another man in old ragged clothes stuck in an iron cage hanging from the wall of an ancient castle. The cruelty with which people were treated in the old days was terrible. It's the replicas of the murderers and the other rogues that show Madame Tussaud's art at its best, and looking at them, it's hard to credit that they are not living and breathing there in front of your eyes. You'd be amazed to find how many of them bear Irish names. It was nice to move up after that and look at the Sleeping Beauty, at her beautiful blonde hair and her breast rising and falling just as if she was alive.

I left the other two in the evening and made my way out to Packie's house where we spent a couple of hours yarning away about Renmore and all that happened while we were soldiering there. I was surprised to find how much I had forgotten about the place since I left it in 1950. There was a time when I was certain that I would never, never forget the great comrades I had there in the army. But, alas! as we go through life, we gradually forget the things that once we loved most.

* An army term for a private.

Many's the man in this country left his father's house in grief and sorrow swearing that he'd never let a week go by without writing to the old folks but who doesn't take up his pen even once a year now!

We passed the evening in *Finsbury Park Tavern*, Packie, myself and Joyce from Ballinakill, quiet and satisfied and not interfering with anybody. But we weren't to get the night all that easy. We were coming out of the public lavatory up at the corner of the park, when the Teddies attacked us. There were seven of them at least, and that I came safely out of the encounter is due to the two companions I had with me.

I suppose the Teddies thought they were away with it when they saw that there were only three of us but, if they did, they were mistaken. Packie gave the biggest fellow the old one-two and you'd have heard the roar out of him, as Packie connected with the jawbone, down at the *Nag's Head*. Then he felled another of them and you can be certain that Joyce wasn't idle all this time. I'm not very much good with my fists but at the same time I haven't a bad grip; so I caught the one nearest to me and got him down on the ground. I was throttling his windpipe when I got a clout on the ear and I had to let him go. I stood up to defend myself and saw Joyce, as spirited as a great hound, giving my man a murderous left hook. Packie was like an old soldier scattering them right and left and at that moment I knew we had won. They raced away down Seven Sister's Road; and we were, in the end, none the worse for the encounter. All that was killing Packie was that they had had the effrontery to attack us at all.

*St. Patrick's Day.* I put a bit of shamrock in the lapel of my coat and went down to Mass in Camden Town at nine o'clock. The church was full and everyone had their bit of shamrock—even some of the Greeks and the Jamaicans, a lot of whom live around those parts. I feel as light-hearted as a lark every St. Patrick's Day and when the congregation started to sing 'Hail Glorious Saint Patrick' my heart swelled out with pride for my race. Hundreds of thousands of people all around the world will be wearing the shamrock today in the Saint's honour and in honour of the country that gave them birth and who can say that the empire that we, the Irish people, have built is not greater and nobler in the four corners of the world than the one that John Bull built with the help of his guns?

You could hardly walk in the street outside the church after Mass, there were so many Irish meeting there and having a bit of sport. Hundreds come up from the country for the Feast-day and most of them don't go back until they have spent all they have. As soon as I got out on the street, I met the MacAndrews and Jim Cannon and great was the welcome we had for one another. We went down to Pano's place for a bite to eat and chewed over the time we were all together working down in Diss in Norfolk. We were dying for the pubs to be open and, as soon as they were, we were into the *Black Cap* like a flash. We laid into the 'stout and mild' with a will and, before long, we all felt nicely enough.

We went down as far as the *Bedford Arms* then as the music is better there than anywhere else. There were so many people in it that it took us all our time to get to the counter. The band was at its best—two violins, an accordion, a concertina, a flute and a couple of those coconut yokes that drummers make noise with; and the lads would let a great wild yell out of them now and again as they got drunk with the music and the booze. I was as bad as any of them myself after a while. I'm like that always when I hear Irish music; even if I have only had one drink, I feel as if I was half-seas over.

Noel and Dympna came looking for me shortly after closing time and I said good-bye to the people from Erris. Hundreds of Irish were outside in the street with the police trying to get them to go along home. We didn't see any trouble but, of course, it was still a bit early in the day. We had dinner in a café on the Edgeware Road and, after that, the three of us went down along to the Park. There were thousands there. It seemed to me that every mother's son of them was wearing the shamrock. Even Matthews, the negro on the African platform, had one of his lapels smothered in shamrock while he had a large paper harp on the other. The same man is very fond of the Irish but very severe on the poor Englishmen.

I passed the afternoon going round and about with Noel and Dympna and didn't leave them until about six o'clock. I drifted over to Finsbury Park where I waited an hour in the *Tavern* for Ward. When it was clear that he wasn't coming, I got the bus down to Camden Town. I pushed my way into the *Laurel Tree*, where most of the Connemara people go and, I need hardly say, it was chockful of them this night. Most of them there were pretty young and spending money as if they had just picked it up off the pavement. I saw one chap carrying a trayful of glasses of whiskey from the counter and he had hardly taken two steps before the whole lot of it was spilt on the floor. There must have been thirty shillings worth in it and wasn't it just a waste of money?

I spent a little time talking to a nice studious man: the rest of the company were getting so lit up that you could get no satisfaction from them at all. Both sides of the bar were jammed tight but, for all that were there, I don't think that a single person was speaking English apart from those behind the counter. Somebody sang a few bars of 'The White Strand' and 'Michael Paddy's Hooker' but some of the younger crowd were beginning to get a bit quarrelsome by this time so, for the sake of my own health, I took myself off.

I went up to the dance in the Galway Social Club in Greenland Street where I met Marcus Joe Barbara and Martin Cooke as soon as I entered the place. They had some nice young dancers over specially from Ireland and the band was superb. I danced the 'Stack of Barley' with a lovely woman from Carna and I went out for the 'Haymaker's Jig' also; but I don't feel as keen on this work as I used to back in Spiddal long ago.

I felt a bit melancholy in the dance-hall after a while and I went out. I don't rightly know what was wrong with me but I couldn't feel any more desire for sport and companionship at all. Whatever came over me, but I felt that I was outside the sport and the pleasure somehow and all of a sudden the whole day palled on me. I walked to King's Cross and got a bus home.

A nice healthy night, thanks be to God.

I lay in bed next morning until ten o'clock and when I went down to get myself a cup of tea, there was a letter from Kevin there telling me to go up to Daventry. He has got a job for me at the building and I can stay with him in his house. I'm sorry to be leaving this place now but I have no call to be staying on any longer for I'll never get anywhere drinking and spending money foolishly.

# 7

# The Kilsby Tunnel

*Daventry, 19.3.1957.* I was sorry to be leaving Ward but I knew that it was for my own good. It took me an hour and three-quarters to get to Northampton and from there I caught a bus to Daventry. There was over a mile to go to Kevin's house so I got a cab for a couple of shillings out to it. They both gave me a great welcome and we sat up very late into the night yarning away. The little girl had grown very big since I last saw her and, as for the son, well, sure he wasn't there at all at that time. I have a room of my own upstairs so that I should be well enough off here for a while. It was the devil and all getting out from under the warm comfortable blankets to get on the back of a motor-bike to go to work. Kevin is working in a factory near the building site and he will take me to work every morning though I'll have to walk home in the evenings as I finish before he does. I handed in my cards and started off straight away. Three and elevenpence halfpenny an hour this crowd, Bernard Sunley & Son Ltd., are paying and over twenty-five shillings a week as a bonus. Most of the men come out from Northampton on the company's buses but a lot of the people from the 'hamlets' around are working here also.

Which doesn't do the job any good, I'm sorry to say, for the countrymen in this area are the ruination of work like this. They have no truck with trade unions and you'd never see them looking for a rise in their pay or seeking better conditions. They used to say that the Irish who came over here long ago ruined the workers' conditions—working for less than the rate and so on—but that can't be said about them today. It's the labourers who leave the farms for the building jobs who do the damage now—them and the Poles.

Pat Ganly and myself were set digging two large holes down at the end of the field and, God knows we needed the work to heat ourselves. It was a real March day with an east wind blowing fiercely across the countryside and I thought it would take the skin off me any minute. The farmers are turning over the green sods with their ploughs leaving long black furrows behind them and the little white lambs are gambolling in the meadows. It's a healthy kind of countryside hereabouts; this is because it's so high above sea-level, needless to say. There were a couple of bad showers after dinner-time but Pat and I settled ourselves in one of the holes, pulled a bit of tarpaulin across its mouth and waited there until the rain passed over. I felt pretty tired out when I had walked the two miles home after the day's work.

Kevin's wife had a fine hot meal ready for me when I got in. I spent a good while playing with young Eileen before she was put to bed. I couldn't get any reaction from the boy at all; but I suppose he is still too young. A paraffin lamp is what is used here to give light as in most of the houses in the English countryside. Some of the Irish people who go home now and again boast about how up to the minute everything is over here but if they told the truth, there are plenty of parts of this country still backward enough. Where do you leave the thatched houses that are as plentiful here around Northampton as they were in Ireland half a century ago—only not half so pretty? What they make the thatch from, I don't know, for I didn't see a lovely golden roof on any of the houses such as you might see back home.

My room has two small windows and I can see the masts and the little red lights of the radio station from one of them. Many's the time I saw 'Daventry' written on the dial of the radio at home but I never thought I'd ever live within an ass's roar of the place. But, as you might guess, the exile never knows where he's going to end up.

Pay day today for the other lads on the job but I won't get a make* until next week and, even then, I'll only get four days' pay. I've often said that it was a rotten thing to keep the first week's pay back until the second week the way they do here in this country. If you can believe them, they do it for the convenience of the pay-clerks but I suspect that there is something else to it as well. Isn't the same money lying in the bank earning interest for the employer concerned?

This job is only starting. They are building a ball-bearing factory and pipes and roads have to be laid before the building starts at all. For a moment, it's navvies that are mostly needed; no tradesmen will be called on for some time. But no one knows where we'll be by that time. On this kind of work, the man who cuts the first sod is seldom around when the last stone is being laid.

Teddy Shanahan from Tipperary is in charge of the navvies and, as far as I can see, nobody could find any fault with him. The weather is dreadful all day today and we had to spend most of the time in the hut. There are plenty of English country-men here—swede-bashers as they are called—and to hear them talking you'd think you were listening to 'The Archers'.

There's a great difference between them and country people in Ireland. I have to say that this crowd are very like the 'yokels' that you come across on funny postcards. Every man of them has a big red face, a slow unintelligent gait of going and a mode of talking as queer as anything you ever heard. They can't converse together without screaming and roaring and you'd think they had the mentality of children. They go on and on about the same thing until anyone listening to them gets browned off with their nonsense. Like this (and I don't exaggerate):

'I'm goin' Banbury a week next Sattidy, George.'

'You ain't, are you?'

'Yis, I am, you know.'

'Cor, you don't arf git about, 'Arry.'

'Well, George, you see what it is, it's when you got a moo'bike, it's easy git around.'

* An Irish colloquialism for a half-penny.

'Yis, 'Arry, you got sumpin' there. When you got the ol'
transport, you can git round about the country, but when you
ain't, you're jiggered. I always say a car or a bike is an 'andy
thing fer gitting around with.'

'I know it is, George.'

On jobs like this, the Irish often take the mickey out of them,
starting nonsensical conversations just to see how long the
English will keep them up. Their line of chat annoys me very
much and I hate to be stuck on a job with any of them. The
labourers in Ireland don't go in for this kind of foolishness at all.
On the contrary. There is spirit and meaning in their conversation coupled with a beauty and range of vocabulary whether
they speak in Irish or in English.

But to be fair to them, I must say that these countrymen
don't bear any kind of grudge against other people as we do,
both amongst ourselves and towards others; and you'd have
more rows in a single day at a hurling match or a fair back in
Ireland than these poor devils would have over a year. If it
was on the likes of these that England was depending for the
building of her Empire, I don't know from God how they
succeeded so well. But, of course, they didn't. There were
plenty of Scots and Irish and tough little Cockneys there to
conquer the poor foreigners for them.

We finished the holes, myself and Pat Ganly, and we had to
get behind the mixer after that. The wind was blowing the
cement about and we were rightly banjaxed by it before long.
It went into our mouths, our eyes and our nostrils until we were
absolutely tormented by it.

Ever since we started off on it, I have had my doubts as to
whether we'll ever get away from that bloody mixer. Two
dumpers were drawing the concrete away from us so that we
were kept going hard—Pat shovelling sand, myself shovelling
stones and Stefan the Pole throwing in the bags. The Pole is a
bit lazy but he's cute enough not to be caught idle no matter
who comes by. It's a long time since I worked so hard but it's
good for me; I feel better already.

Who do you think came along looking for work but Martin
O'Toole from Spiddal? He was taken on without any bother,
needless to say, as he's a first-class man. I'm glad he's starting

here for I'll hear a few words of Irish now and again. I didn't hear any since I left London.

I told Kevin's wife not to bother getting a meal ready for me in the evenings. They have their own dinner in the middle of the day and between looking after the children and the other household chores, it would be asking too much of the poor woman to have another meal ready for me in the evenings. I can always prepare a bite for myself.

I brought a bit of trout home with me this evening and boiled it in milk. The couple in this house never look at fish like most other Irish people and it's a great mistake. There's nothing as nice as a piece of fish but, somehow or other, the Irish have a great resistance to it. They prefer all the time to go for bacon or beef and don't they look like it—half of them suffering from blood pressure. It wasn't on red meat that the Aran Islanders lived and where would you get as strong and as healthy a community as they are?

I didn't go out at all tonight and I won't venture out for a while yet, with the help of God. I'm going to be very careful now and, indeed, I have to after my three weeks or thereabouts back in London with Ward and the other loonies. Kevin came in early from work and I looked after the house while Eileen and himself went off to the Rosary. I'm sitting in great comfort by the fire, writing this in the lamplight and nothing to be heard but the tick-tock of the clock and the murmur of the wind against the gable of the house. Maybe it's a nice thing to be married, in a way?

Most of the men went off home at twelve o'clock but I stayed on working until four. Time and a half is the rate from twelve o'clock on Saturday and double time if you work on Sunday. That, of course, is what the trade union has laid down. There's no Sunday work here so far but I expect there will be in due course.

We found the afternoon dragged very much as we hadn't all that much to do once the other men went home. I bought some beef on the way home and roasted it with an onion. Daventry is not much of a place; most of the people go into Northampton twelve miles away to do their shopping and, indeed, there weren't many to be seen around today.

A couple of letters awaited me when I got home, one from Father Eric and another from Patrick Dollart. Both of them had been addressed to me in Irish and Eileen told me that the postman had enquired if she had a Hungarian staying in the house. I'm telling you that if I'm staying on here for a while, he'll recognise Irish when he sees it.

For the matter of that, there have been a good few Hungarians around here since the Rising and the natives, since they got to know them properly, don't care for them all that much. Just before Christmas, the people in one of the villages nearby made a house available for a Hungarian family that had escaped. The villagers filled the house with furniture and laid on a store of food and coal for the family also. You'd imagine that the poor exiles that had suffered so much would be thankful for all this; but no, it was quite otherwise. They stayed in the house for one night only and then went into Northampton to inform the authorities there that they wanted a house in the city since they weren't used to country life.

I was in digs myself with some of them in Northampton and, from what I saw of them, I didn't think they were very willing to put up with much in the way of privation. They were all dressed nicely and, although we had the best of good food in that house, they were never satisfied. From beginning to end they were complaining and grousing. I'm not saying that they haven't as much right as anyone else to kick up a row but you'd think that, after suffering so much hardship and deprivation in their own country, they would be prepared to put up with a few little difficulties here and there. At the same time, we have to pray to God that none of us have ever to suffer the amount of cruelty and persecution that they had to put up with from the Russians.

I walked into Daventry and said a couple of prayers in the church there. It's only a little chapel for there aren't many Catholics hereabouts. There were a few people gathered together at the corner and I thought of home and how the boys would be gathered at a similar corner commenting on anyone that passed by. But this crowd are not at all like the groups that collect at the corners in Ireland. They have no conversation other than what can be said in short sharp sentences. To listen to them, you'd be convinced that they knew no word of two syllables or more. They perpetually chew gum like cows chewing the cud and I doubt if they ever have any thought that wouldn't equally occur to a cow.

I drifted into the *Lion and the Lamb* and had a bottle of Guinness. There was a good crowd in there making so much noise that you'd think they were drinking barrels of beer—which they weren't. They're a close crowd, these country people, and even though they go into the pub now and again, they stretch out each drink so long that it's a wonder the landlord gets any profit at all. The pubs in England are kept beautifully clean, the floorboards and every bit of wood well-scrubbed and they have all sorts of things to entice customers in: music, darts, skittles and crib and even television in some of the places. You could pass the whole night dallying over a drink or two and you'd never be told that you should be drinking more than you are doing. The pub here is a meeting-place for the people, or for some of them, and parish questions are often hammered out in them. But the pubs in Ireland have two advantages that English pubs will never have and those same advantages are: the quality of the conversations and the quality of the drink.

Off for Mass in Daventry at eleven. Father Collins gave a good sermon. He's a great talker, God bless him, and he has a nice direct approach so that you feel he's talking specially to you.

I walked down the fields to the reservoir after dinner. Wouldn't it be nice to have a little rowing boat and go out on the water for an hour or two? But even if you had the same, it's not permitted. Ah! when I think of the Corrib and the lovely days I spent on it rowing away with the water making sweet music lapping against the sides of the boat with the ruined walls of Menlo Castle guarding the mouth of the lake and the mountains to the north alight with the setting sun! Coming back then at night to the quayside with the drought growing on you every minute. A few drinks in the *Brooklyn Bar* with Patsy Lydon and other old friends and a feed of crubeens in Pigfoot Pat's place on your way back to Renmore. That's when life had a flavour but, alas, we weren't lucky enough for it to have lasted.

I noticed a rabbit or two on the way back. They took a terrible beating, the poor creatures, for no reason at all. But treachery is always repaid and, from what I hear the farmers are no better off as a result of their campaign against the rabbits since the foxes and stoats have wreaked havoc among the hens and ducks since the rabbit population disappeared. And, despite them, the rabbits will be back.

I started to read *Good-bye, Mr. Chips*, in the afternoon and I must admit that I haven't enjoyed a book so much for a long time. The narrative is wonderful throughout, particularly the piece about the old master who saw the years 'like lazy cattle drifting across the landscape,' and it left me regretful for a life that I had never known beyond reading about it. Words are a marvellous medium and in the hands of the man that wrote *Good-bye, Mr. Chips*, with his sparing artistic use of them, they can create a world for you that you cannot forget as long as you live.

Kevin and Eithne went off to the pictures tonight. It's well worth their while having someone in the house to look after the children while they escape for an hour or two at night.

Lamplight is a poor substitute for electricity.

I ran into a couple of Irishmen who told me that a big job was starting in a railway tunnel outside Rugby and that a good many men would be needed. I was in two minds as to what was best for me to do but in the end I went along to Rugby to see about it.

The tunnel is about two miles out from Rugby Central and when I get along to it there was a good crowd in front of me all after the same thing. An agent and a clerk were there taking down names as fast as they could and, without much delay, I made my way up to the front. They didn't want to start me when I hadn't got my cards in my fist but I told them I'd fetch them without delay and so I got the job. Seventeen pounds a week they are paying but we have to work from half-past seven in the morning until six o'clock in the evening for the whole seven days of the week. It will give me a chance to get a few quid together.

Who did I meet but the Gannons, Pat and Andrew and Charlie O'Malley. I could hardly credit my eyes as I was under the impression that these lads weren't nearer than a hundred miles of this place. We had a great welcome for each other and we all went down together to the mouth of the tunnel where the gangs were being made up.

We were put under an old skin from Lancashire that we baptised 'Handlebars' as soon as we laid eyes on him. You wouldn't have seen anything like him since Buffalo Bill that we used to read about long ago. He sported a big wide hat and a leather jacket, a huge belt around his middle and corduroy breeches that were tied under his knees with cords or 'yorks' as the navvies call them. On either side of his mouth there were at least six inches of moustache and a huge drop-bowl pipe hanging out from under them. He looked us over in an irritated sort of way as if he didn't want us at all—which I suppose he didn't—and beckoned us to follow him.

We went in under the dark arch of the tunnel and, inside, it was quite unlike what it appeared to be from the outside. A long chain of lights hung from the walls, each light about fifty yards from the other; it was as black as pitch between them and the dust and smoke would choke you. What was worse, there was a dreadful noise from the bull-dozers that were being filled and emptied; while, as well as all that, the noise of the pneumatic drills battering away would deafen you. New drains are being put in all along the tunnel and new ballast under the rails.

The first thing we had to do was to empty wagons of ballast and we had enough on our plates with that. It wasn't too bad as you neared the floor of the wagon but, until then, it was the devil's own job trying to drive the shovels down through the ballast. To make it worse, the dust was rising up in huge clouds choking and blinding us until we were properly fed up with the whole thing. But what put us out most of all was that we had no chance to have a decent chat after our long separation; however, Handlebars was watching us too carefully and none of us wanted to draw him down on us too soon.

He blew the whistle at last, at all events, telling us that it was time for the tea and I tell you, we were thankful for it by then. The tea man came by with two large buckets of tea and a box full of paper cups like what you get on the boat from Dun Laoire. He gave each man a drink. We badly needed it, the same drink, but another man came along after the tea man with a basket of food out of which he gave something to every man. I've worked on many a job but I never saw this caper on any one of them before. The sandwiches were wrapped in paper and were superb—beef, ham, cheese and a little currant cake as well—and we didn't say yes or no to the chap that handed them to us in case he was making a mistake; we just laid into them with a will. Handlebars blew his whistle again immediately the ten minutes were up. Back to the shovelling we went but we were well revived after the good snack and we didn't find the work so hard from then on.

We had a great chat at dinner-time and the lads mentioned everything that had happened to them since we had separated down in Norfolk almost three years ago. They are digging in Northampton and the Company bus brings them out every morning. Two buses come from Coventry also and one from Leicester. I'm thinking of moving into Northampton too. I find the country too quiet.

There are odd fellows on the job here and that's no more than the truth. You wouldn't know where they came from unless they were fired out of the unemployment exchange by the poor clerks who got fed up at them perpetually begging away. One of them I recognized as a man who used to collect the empty glasses in a pub in Northampton. He wore an overcoat that was far and away too long for him with a huge pin holding it together at the neck; and for all that he did, he might as well not been there at all.

There was another half-eejit that had just arrived over from County Derry. Drumsurn, I thought he called the place and he was as queer a lad as you ever saw. Three playboys from Maghera were there pulling his leg and, really, you'd have to laugh at them. The man from Drumsurn hadn't an idea between himself and his God as to how he had come across from Ireland. His cousin had come with him and had guided him. The other crowd asked him whether he had come by Dun Laoire or by Heysham but he couldn't enlighten them. In the end, he got a bit annoyed and he retorted: 'Youse Maghera boys are very Englified. Youse think youse are smart but youse'll not put anything over on me.' I had to laugh at that for the crowd that were taking the mickey out of him were as Irish as you could come across. Not only that but they dislike the English intensely; which those of us who come from the South don't.

Then there was another big buck—a fine strong man to tell you the truth—from the north of Scotland and if he hadn't been let out of a looney bin, well, I couldn't guess where he had come from. All he was worrying about was where would he get a job looking after sheep, and, while he'd be talking to you, he's have a kind of lost distrait look in his big eyes. He spoke quietly and civilly, like someone that had been well-schooled and I think he has plenty of Scots Gaelic if he'd only take the trouble to speak it. He gave me the Gaelic words for a lot of things but I don't know whether he could sustain a conversation in Gaelic or not.

There was another little buck of a Lithuanian there and he was seven times worse, at least, than any of the other three. He didn't like anyone to come near him, even the 'general' himself as he came around, and he kept talking away to himself all the time he was working. Handlebars himself tried to get him to move in nearer to the gang and not to be digging away on his own so far from the rest of us. Didn't your man start giving out then about 'dictators' and communists and all sorts of things until poor Handlebars, God love him, was up the spout altogether. He left the buck on his own thereafter and had nothing to do with him for the rest of the day.

The tunnel is more than a mile long and there are two shafts to let the smoke and the gas escape. Two gangs are working outside in the clean air mixing concrete and the concrete is let down through the air-shafts to those who are levelling it out. No one from the railways is working in here except the diesel driver and his mate and, according to what we're told, the railway workers don't particularly like a private company having this job. But, there you are, if the job depended on the railway workers, it would be a long time getting done.

In this country, a lot of the work on the railways is done by private firms and it seems that the workers live in old wagons and get their own meals for themselves. One gang of fifty men are working for Proctor of Manchester and every man jack of them, from the boss down to the cook, is from the Aran Islands. They work non-stop from Saturday night until Sunday afternoon and get a huge pay-packet. I know some of them myself and it's seldom they go out anywhere, except for the very odd time, so that they can save a good deal of money. It's easy for them to go home after a few years here and buy a little place for themselves. And good luck to them!

I gave Eithne five pounds to send home to the old lady and two pounds for herself. I don't need very much in this place: there's little on which I could spend it.

We were furious this morning when we had to refuse the lovely sandwiches because it was Friday; though, indeed, there are many Irishmen that don't fulfil their obligations as they should. They have respect neither for the Fast nor for Friday. We worked very hard filling wagons with old ballast that the carters brought to us. It was harder to handle than the new stuff even though no dust arose from it. All sorts of dirt was mixed up with it and, by the time the tea man came along, we had hardly any appetite left.

These Erris people are great workers. They'd spend the whole day bent over shovelling stones without getting anyway tired. No matter what kind of work they're given, they're able for it: farming, navvying or anything else.

This tunnel is hell in a way—you haven't the comfort in it that you might have outside. It's pitch dark, the air is always humid and the walls weep so that you'd think, at times, that you were looking at waterfalls. The place is full of black diesel smoke from morning to night what with the wagons, the small shunting engines and the compressors that are as big as asscarts back home.

We got a bit of a respite in the afternoon when Handlebars told us to go and give a hand to Bill Donovan who wanted help at the air-shaft to move the mixer about. When we came out of the muck and the dirt, we were nearly blinded with the gorgeous sunlight and, as for the nice fresh air, well, we thought it strange that it should be there at all. We had a long walk across the fields to reach the mixer and we were like boys let off school on a sunny afternoon, we were so pleased with ourselves. It was then I regretted the lovely healthy job I had thrown up back in Daventry.

We stretched out the little job as far as we could, I'm telling you, and I think the foreman was as bad as we were for he made no complaint about our slowness. The three who normally worked on the mixer were in a hurry and wanted to get the mixer moved as quickly as possible but we kept the rein on them in spite of them. I recognized one of them—a mean little fellow from Wales that ruins any job he's on, running to the foreman with tittle-tattle tales and trying to make out that he's a good man. I don't know why on earth people back home in Ireland keep writing to the papers and giving lectures about the relationship between ourselves and the Welsh—as if it was anything to be proud of. I met a good few of them and I saw nothing in them that was worth boasting about. The reputation they have here amongst all sorts is that they are a people that can't be trusted and that the bulk of them are always currying favour. At all events, I don't see why a fine vigorous nation that had fought the English as we did has to have anything to do with that crowd.

Eventually, we had to go back to the tunnel but it took us a good while to cover the road. As we entered under the tunnel, it was like going into Hell after a vision of Heaven. Handlebars was there with his big leather coat thrown on one side as he wrestled with a lump of wood trying to lever an old drain-pipe into place. When he finished, there was a huge pile of dirt all around and we had to fall to and shovel it up into the wagons. We were up to our ankles in this filth and each time we flung a shovelful into the wagon some of it always fell back down on us. It was a bit like that other job back in Edmonton except that Handlebars wasn't as bad as Mike Sheehan.

The days are getting a bit of a stretch now, thank God, and it won't be long until the wind and the rain are gone. I let Kevin and Eithne go along into the Rosary tonight while I stayed behind and looked after the children. It's nice and soothing to sit by the fire at night-time listening to the clock on the wall while the lamp flings pictures on the ceiling with every move you make. There must be traces of the hermit in me for I'm well content to be alone half the time without seeing a single soul.

We found out today why we get sandwiches every morning on this job. It seems that the contractors get subsistence money from the railway company for every man employed here and instead of paying it over to each man, they arranged for these snacks to be supplied. It's a dirty trick, surely. The two pounds nine would add a tidy bit to the wage-packet but we can't do anything about it. There's no union or any association here to help us stand up for our rights.

We had great crack at dinner-time today. It all started with an old magazine that had been thrown aside by someone. It was filled with pictures of the glamour girls that you see on the movies and Andrew and Charles O'Malley began to go through it picking their choices. They were very matey to begin with.

'Show me the one that you'd like best, Charlie,' said Andrew.

'You work away,' said Charlie, 'take your choice first.'

The matiness didn't last very long. Both of them coveted Ava Gardner and then the trouble started!

'Isn't it well that you'd want that one,' said Andrew, getting sulky.

'To hell with you,' said Charlie, 'haven't I as much right to her as you have?'

'I picked her first,' answered Andrew.

'Ah, you were just the same down in Peterboro' when you tried to take Mary Sweeney off me,' shouted Charlie.

'By God, it was easy to take her off you. She didn't fancy you at all, if you had only known it.'

'Who? She didn't fancy me, indeed! And why wouldn't she fancy me? Wasn't she cracked about me altogether, you devil?'

Well, they started off and slanged one another about everything that had happened to them from the time they first met. In the end, they nearly came to blows. Pat O'Brien and myself

were knocking ourselves out listening to them. What harm but
the dialect the two of them speak! They are both from Erris
and they speak a strange kind of Irish.

'Yis are a great pair,' grinned Pat who was getting right
sport out of the whole scene.

In the end, I solved the problem myself when I mentioned
that the good lady they had been arguing about couldn't come
within an ass's roar of Marilyn Monroe. At this, they gave
over squabbling and started to compare the attractions of the
various Hollywood ladies. They got on good terms again within
a few minutes and Pat said: 'Well, the devil take both of you
and God look down on anyone that would pay any attention to
either of you.' By this time, Handlebars had the whistle in his
fist so we had to forget the luscious ladies in the magazine and
seize hold of our respective implements once again.

Handlebars is an amazing creature. He's a good example, I
would think, of the traditional type of foreman that you would
find on this kind of job before the war. Interested in nothing
but the work itself and the pub, they dress in a manner they
accept as being laid down for their kind—moleskin or corduroy
trousers, a scarf tied round their necks and a cap or a hat that
is only taken off going to bed, if at all. Most of them are Irish
but a lot come from the north of England also.

I felt a bit played out as I got home this evening, not so much
from the amount of work I had done as from a kind of depression that had got hold of me. As I washed and shaved, I began
to feel better and I walked into Daventry. I said a prayer or
two in the church and afterwards knocked back a couple of pints
in the *Plough and Bell*. The back room was full of half-frozen
old fellows watching each other to see who would be first to
stand a half-pint all round. They're a queer crowd, the Midlands people, without any 'go' or spunk in them and living
rather meanly. Any ordinary workman back home in Ireland
in a pub on a Saturday night would say: 'To hell with it!
Knock it back! We're alive, aren't we?'

God knows, if at home they had the money and the comfort
people have here, there's not a country would be better for
sheer enjoyment of life. Kevin and Eithne were safely asleep
when I got home. Isn't it a poor enough life they have, from

bed to work and back again and none of the small comforts that a young married couple might be entitled to expect?

Thoroughly fed up with myself today for some reason. I suppose having to work on Sunday is the reason for this feeling for, although I've done it before, I never really feel right about it.

Andrew didn't come along to work today. He's in a bad income tax bracket unlike most of the lads and if he came working today, he'd have little to show for his Sunday. Plenty of the Irish working over here don't pay income tax at all—they pretend to have a wife and children back home in Ireland. I suppose the Tax people find it hard to prove whether that is the case or not, but, at all events, they do little enough about it. Now and again, a man is caught and he gets a prison sentence or a stiff fine; it's worth taking the chance, however, for if you cough up the way you're supposed to, there wouldn't be any point in having any kind of lucrative job at all.

For instance, the chap earning fifteen pounds a week—and earning it the hard way, more than likely—wouldn't have in his pay-packet more than twelve pounds or thereabouts when tax and insurance is deducted. That doesn't encourage men to get on the building jobs or suchlike; and any man that has a bad code-number, you may be sure that he doesn't bother working more than five days. Some time ago, an Irish reporter came over to investigate the way the Irish lived here and a tax inspector that he interviewed in Glasgow said to him: 'There must be more than ten million people living in the Irish Republic because, according to the forms I have here, nearly every person of the age of eighteen upwards or so has over five of a family at home.' Alas! this is not the case. Instead of expanding, the Irish nation is getting smaller.

I was working with another gang today for an hour or two where help was needed to get a couple of loads of pipes out of the wagons. Three of the people I was with were from Galway City and they lived in Coventry. By all accounts, you'd be hard put to find any difference between the two cities, so many Galway people are in Coventry. I think people from the towns in Ireland settle down here in England quicker than people from the Irish countryside but that's probably because they're used to city life.

I had hardly time to get a bit to eat after work as I had to get along to Northampton to attend the Workers' Mass at half-past eight there. I went up to the Club afterwards as there was a dance being held there. Plenty of good-looking girls come along to the dances there. At home, you wouldn't get a dance being held during the whole of Lent but here, nothing is thought of it. The Church runs the Club and the dances and if it wasn't for the money they make out of them, they'd find it hard to build schools for the children of the exiles as they get little enough help from the State.

There's nothing much to the dance that takes place here but it keeps the Catholics together and that makes it worthwhile. Only one thing ruins the effort being made here and that is the fighting which takes place, I am afraid, frequently enough. Drink is mostly responsible, I need hardly say, and the priests who are here now haven't the same control as Father Galvin used to have. He thought nothing of going along and throwing out the rowdies just like you'd throw out a dog that had soiled the floor. It's a terribly bad example these bucks give as they fight and beat one another up outside the club (and only thirty yards from the church at that) and all because they have a couple of pints under their belts. They let down both their country and their faith but they're so thick and so ignorant that they aren't even conscious of that fact.

I came across a nice girl from Cashel during the 'Siege of Ennis' and I had a long chat with her after that dance. Like a lot of people from those parts, her command of Irish wasn't as good as if she had come from the real Gaeltacht but, at the same time, she didn't break into English at all. I could have taken her away from the dance, I think, but for the fact that I had to catch the last bus back to Daventry. Damn the place! There's no satisfaction for me in it at all.

The first of April, the Fool's Day. First thing this morning, Andrew challenged me to go and tell Handlebars that the General was looking for him up at the office but when I saw the state he was in after his night's drinking, I was afraid to go near him at all never mind about pulling his leg!

A lot of men were away from work today. It's a kind of practice here—to work Sunday and stay home Monday. They'll be in the *Admiral Rodney* drinking and playing darts until closing time and probably moving off to the Bookie after that.

We were laying pipes as hard as we could and it was a dirty enough job for the trench was completely water-logged. To give Handlebars his due, he knows his job and when he undertakes anything, you can be sure that it will be well done. He managed to get rid of that little Lithuanian and pass him on to Bill Donovan when Bill needed a new man. 'Here, you can have this chap and welcome,' Handlebars said to the Corkman with a slight smile at the corners of his mouth. The Lithuanian was rightly worked up when he found that he was being transferred from our little group:

'You make like dictator, everybody pushing, after all make level,' (whatever that meant). 'I no like when everybody speak for me: "you come here, you go there", similar donkey. Why you no speak for Irishman, him go. I think you maybe fraid for him.'

Handlebars found it hard enough to get rid of him and I doubt if Bill Donovan will be all that happy when he finds what he's got. He certainly won't be as patient with him as Handlebars was. Indeed, if it wasn't that work was so plentiful just now, the Lithuanian would hardly find employment at all. But I suppose few knew how much these poor devils went through during the war between concentration camps and the rest: it's no wonder they're a bit odd.

Read *Fód a Bháis* tonight. It's amazing how pure Maire's* Irish is, even allowing for the fact that he was born and reared with it. There are a few like him such as Mairtin Ó Cadhain and Pádraig Óg Ó Conaire to name but two; but there are many others whose writings bear the mark of the English language. It's understandable, I need hardly say; that English must have a certain influence on Irish nowadays since the languages have been struggling together and living side by side since Strongbow's time. And for that matter, the Irish language has left its own mark on the English spoken in Ireland. But reading some of the Irish written today, you'd imagine the

* An Irish author.

writer was doing his best to translate word for word from English into Irish—but then who am I to talk, seeing that I'm as bad as the rest of them.

But over and above that, I doubt if any Irish speaker can keep his language as pure as might be desirable seeing that so much of his life has to be spent among English speakers. The terms and the images native to the English language are affecting the Irish language and corrupting it and you always have to be on the lookout to make sure that the real idiom is not escaping you. Even people from the part of Connemara where nothing but Irish is spoken, find their Irish corrupted after a while over here. Often enough, I have heard them say: 'reveáil suas an t-engine sin' (rev up that engine) or 'Handáil anuas agam an pipe-coll ar sin mar a dhéanfadh fear maith' (hand me that pipe-collar like a good man). I suppose this sort of thing can't be helped when Irish speakers are dealing with things that hitherto have had no philological equivalent in Irish.

We saw the last of Handlebars today when we were sent up to the north mouth of the tunnel where a gang was working under an ill-mannered buck from County Mayo. We were thoroughly dismayed when we heard how he was roaring and yelling all the time. Nobody could satisfy him, it seemed. Three wagons of concrete pipes came along with each pipe weighing about a hundredweight and, when we started to lift them out of the wagons at two men to a pipe, he nearly burst with rage.

'Two men to carry one of those things,' he bellowed, 'I'd lift one of them with my little finger on a bad day. I don't know what kind of shrimps they're sending over from Mary Horan's* since the war. When I came over, they were sending men not women.'

With that, he grabbed one of the pipes and swung it up over his head just as if it had been a sod of peat. If you only saw the arms that man had when he took hold of the pipe with the muscles standing out like huge thick ropes, you'd say that no man on earth could ever stand up to him. But, let me tell you, that's what happened. An Englishman, by God, spoke up and said: I don't think there's any necessity for that kind of carry

* Ireland.

on, Pat. The lads are doing the job well enough. You're not back in the depression times, you know.'

Your man could hardly credit that anyone in the gang would have the nerve to speak to him like that. He laid down his burden just as you'd lay down your cup and said to the man:

'Are you telling me how to run this gang?'

'No, Pads,' said the Englishman—and I knew from the 'Pads' that he was from the West country. 'I was only saying that there's no need to come the bully on the fellows.'

'Well, keep your gob shut in the future or I'll close it for you sharpish,' your man roared as he grabbed the pipe again.

'You don't speak to me like that, Pads,' the little man replied and there was a new edge to his voice as he said it.

The foreman turned on him like a wild animal.

'I'll stick your head to the bloody wall, you sow-dog,' he yelled, grinding his teeth with rage.

'O.K., then,' the Englishman said evenly, 'come out in the air.'

Out in the air they went and I'm afraid I have to say that every man jack of us went out with them to see what was going to happen. There wasn't a word out of anybody and we all just watched. The little man took up a defensive attitude and looked at the bully. I never in my life saw anybody less afraid than he was.

The foreman let a roar like a bull out of him and made a sudden rush at the little Englishman. All the Englishman did was to step to one side and let 'Pads' have one on the nose that brought the blood spurting out through his nostrils. The Mayoman let another roar out of him but you could sense the pain in it this time and he made another dive for where he thought the Englishman ought to be. The West country man made the same ploy but it was full in the mouth that he hit the foreman this time. He then started dancing around like a fairy and we knew that he was knowledgeable about the fighting game. If the bully could only have caught him, there's no doubt but that murder would have been done but the Englishman kept a safe distance between himself and his tormentor.

I don't know what would have happened but the general came along just then when no one was expecting him. He was rightly worked up when he saw what was going on and he threatened everyone with the sack straight away, the foreman included. But this much good came out of the whole affair— he sent the foreman off down the tunnel to another gang and we were left for the rest of the day to empty the wagons.

I had a chance later to talk to the chap who had roughed up the foreman.

'I'm really sorry it had to be one of your chaps, Pads,' he said to me. 'Why, I've worked all over England and Wales with you Irish chaps and I've always been good friends with them.'

Indeed, no one could have blamed the Englishman for the fight. It was forced on him but he didn't flinch from it.

When we got in to work in the morning, there was no foreman put in place of the other fellow but the gang was split and distributed among the other gangs. We walked down the whole length of the tunnel from the north end but no one interfered with us at any stage. Even our old friend Handlebars didn't try to get us working. I was there with Andrew and Charlie—the rest of the gang were working here and there down the tunnel and we didn't rightly know what we should do. Some lack of co-ordination was responsible for our being left to ourselves and I think that every foreman we met thought we belonged to some gang or other.

Well, we didn't mind; we weren't kicking up any row about that. The clerk had taken our names during the morning so that we'd be paid even if we did nothing except walk around until evening. So, as a result, when we had our tea and sandwiches, we decided that we'd spend some time wandering around before we got to thinking about work.

We made our way up to the north of the tunnel again and nobody created any difficulty about it. That's when we thought of going out.

'Let's leave this for a while,' said Andrew, 'we'll get out into the air.'

Charlie and I were a bit afraid that we'd be caught if we strolled too far away from the tunnel when we had no reason for doing so but we gave way to Andrew and out we went. We felt like a group of schoolboys 'mitching' from school as we made our way up through the wood. We enjoyed the 'jag' for a while but eventually the idleness got us down and we made our way back to the tunnel and the labouring. Just like the horse that is accustomed to work, we all get contrary when we take it too easy.

I was right when I guessed that Bill Donovan wouldn't take too kindly to that little Lithuanian. He'd been annoyed by him ever since he accepted him into his gang but today he really couldn't put up with him any longer. Anything he said, the little buck turned into a horror story, and began to nag and complain and threaten revenge and bad luck on everyone in the gang as a result. He thinks everybody is down on him though they happen to spend most of their time listening to him. Bill Donovan, anyway, told this gobdaw, that he'd have to give over what he was at—scraping away with the shovel like an old hen picking—and help the rest of the gang to move the wagons full of ballast a few yards down the line.

'You make for me like dictator,' the buck squealed, 'all the time speak for me! Why you no speak for other peoples?' and he went on with a stream of vituperation in his own language. Donovan was pretty fed up by this time.

'Well, the Lord keep my hands off you,' he roared as he began to feel nasty. The Lithuanian mustn't have seen that he was in danger of death or, if he did, he didn't care. He kept on giving out as much as he could but he didn't finish his sentence this time. The Corkman grabbed him by the back of the neck and lifted him off the ground. He walked over to the drain in which they were laying the pipes. There was about six inches of water in the drain and the Lithuanian was very nearly being dumped down in it. All the time, he was trying to free himself from the big man's grip but it was no good. You could only compare it to a fly in the grip of the fly-paper. Another minute and he'd have been flung down in the water but, by God's grace, the boss came along just then.

Bill Donovan turned on him: 'Here, get this fellow out of my sight or I'll murder him before long! A saint himself couldn't put up with him! Get him out of my sight before I do something that I'll be sorry for.'

The Lithuanian seems to have a bad reputation all around

the place because the boss signalled to the buck to follow him and the little gnat did that with a will. The camp will be a happy enough place now for a little while.

But sure, what harm. That sort of thing shortens the day for us.

I told Kevin tonight that I was thinking of looking for digs in Northampton. He doesn't like to think of me leaving for they seldom meet anyone from home; but I'd have a better time in town.

I drew fifteen pounds today when they went around with the pay. I'll send ten pounds home to my mother and give two to Kevin's wife. I'll have enough left to see me through.

# 8

# Three Playboys

———◆◆◆———

*Saturday, 6.4.1957.* I took a day off from the tunnel and went into Northampton on my own. I went up to Victor Rajczonek's house where I stayed before Christmas and, as luck would have it, the woman of the house had a place for me.

'Ah, Danny, you like coming back to my house? Such nice Irish boys I now have! They never making trouble, very little drink.'

From the way she spoke, you think she had a gang of teetotallers lodging with her.

The city looked a bit strange to me having been so long away from it but I won't be long getting used to it. Sometimes, I think that Northampton has got a grip on me for no matter how far I stray, I always arrive back there. Two years ago I went to Doncaster up in Yorkshire and I thought I'd never see Northampton again; but I did. From Doncaster I moved to Huntingdon and from there to London, and to Watford and then back to Northampton.

It's not that there's anything there. God knows, there's not as much life there as there is in Galway City. But it attracts you all the same. I've heard many an Irishman say the same thing. Its main advantage is that it is a nice quiet place that's not too far from London or Birmingham and it has plenty of nice public parks. If you were stoney broke on a summer's day, you could go into any of the parks and lie flat on your back looking at the blue sky over you while you listened to the sleepy sound of the willow meeting the ball. God knows, I know nothing whatever about the game but somehow or other there's great peace wherever it's being played.

I dropped into the *Admiral Rodney* about midday and there was a good crowd of the lads there. I was surprised to notice how many of those who worked in the tunnel didn't bother going to work today. And, after all, they pay time and a half for Saturday work! I'll bet that few enough will be missing tomorrow.

The Irish have been going to the *Rodney* for a long time now. The English foregather in one part while the Irish get together in the front and they don't mix at all. It's mostly piece-workers who frequent this place and all you hear them talking about is where the best farmers are, where is the beet being pulled or thinned or what are they paying nowadays for the potato pickers. The Irish at home, so far as I know, haven't got this ugly habit—always talking about work and money—but they get as materialistic as the rest when they have been here awhile. I've often been with workmen in a pub in Ireland and we always had plenty to talk about besides the daily job. They had all the best stories and traditional lore at the tips of their tongues—as you might expect of the Irish—but this crowd are interested in nothing beyond jobs and horses. What harm but most of them are from the West of Ireland!

I ran into three lads from County Mayo and, when closing time came, we mosied down to the *Cattle Market Tavern* beside the Cattle Mart where they had an hour's extra time because of the market. The place was full of farmers all wearing coats like what shop assistants wear at home. I never saw any farmers wearing the likes in Ireland and they're all the better for it. The clothing that country people around Galway had long ago was, I always thought, wonderful. Nice white báinín, frieze breeches and a wide hat like a Spaniard's. But, alas! that clothing is going out even back in Connemara today.

In the *Cattle Market Tavern*, the farmers and the labourers (most of them Irish) make their arrangements much as they used to do on Spalpeen* Saturday in Galway—except that over here the spalpeens are in a position to demand good terms from the bosses.

I didn't hang around town much during the afternoon but I made my way home to my brother. Neither himself nor Eithne liked to see me moving off and I had to promise that I wouldn't let a week go by without looking them up.

I brought my bag with me this morning so that I could go straight to the new digs after work. I felt kind of lonely leaving Kevin's house, between saying good-bye to the children and other things but it can't be helped now, anyway.

We worked very hard all day shovelling the ballast out of the wagons while the dry dust choked us all the time. The devil himself would be better company than the same dust; I suffer from hoarseness and shortness of breath if I get too much of it. It couldn't be healthy, that's one sure thing. As long as I live, I'll never forget this place with its perpetual darkness, the sour taste of the smoke in my mouth and the drips of water constantly falling down from the roof of the tunnel. I found the afternoon very long-drawn-out and the man next to me had me moidered asking every other minute what was the time.

There was a good crowd at Mass this evening. I went to the dance in the club hoping to see the girl from Cashel but she wasn't there.

I spent a half an hour this morning bawling at those two devils, Andrew and Charlie, trying to get them out of bed while herself was roaring up at us that the breakfast was on the table. I don't know how some people can sleep so heavily at all. They should be left to sleep for a couple of days and I bet you they'd get up then. They depend a lot on others who find getting up easy and they don't make any effort on their own behalf.

We spent the day with those old concrete pipes carrying them and laying them in place for the other two who were actually laying them. The ground hereabouts is very wet and, of course, that's why the tunnel is so humid and damp. It must

---

* Spalpeens: farm labourers offering themselves for hire.

be a hundred years since it was built and there's no doubt but that it was a great undertaking at that time when all they had was picks and shovels and horse-drawn carts to carry the clay away. The bull-dozer was unknown at that time and they had no mechanical diggers to tear the ground asunder. They had to use wooden props all the time to hold up the walls of the trench or the cut. They say that eight contractors went broke on this tunnel and that they used to have to call out the soldiers from Rugby to control the navvies who were always rebelling against the conditions. The poor devils, all they were looking for was their right, and bad enough that was, but I suppose that the wealthy ones only regarded them as wild animals.

Well, that day went and this day is here and you can be sure that such treatment wouldn't be meted out today. The thanks for that is due to the trades unions. But for them we wouldn't be able to raise our heads. And, for all that, you'll still hear fools saying: 'What good is it to be in the union? What do they get for you?' If the likes of them had a titter of wit, they'd realize that but for the unions they'd have nothing and that, only for the unions, people even today would have the lives of dogs.

The man laying the pipes sent three of us down the tunnel for a bag of cement. He only wanted enough to make a small amount of mortar—water and cement mixed together to go between the joints—but the bags were so far away that one man couldn't manage to bring one down by himself. A man from Northampton and Callaghan from Limerick came with me. Anyhow, the Englishman started to talk about the way we spoke Irish—that is to say, Andrew, Charlie and myself. He began to enquire whether much was spoken in Ireland and so forth. Well, before I could answer the good man, didn't the Limerickman shove in his oar.

'Oh, not at all,' he said, 'it's a dead language but they're trying to revive it.'

'What do you mean, it's a dead language?' said the Englishman. 'Old Paddy here and his mates speak it like ruddy Chinese all day, so it can't be a dead language.'

'Good man, yourself, Limey' I muttered under my breath.

'Only a few people speak it in backward places,' said the knave then.

What harm but he's man well-regarded for the amount of schooling and teaching that he got. I thought that I'd have to explain the position myself to the Northampton man and try not to be too inaccurate about it at the same time. I didn't want him to think that only a few people knew the language as the Limerickman was trying to tell him.

'Well, it's like this,' I said to him, 'unfortunately, it's not as widely spoken as it used to be. But there's a reason for that. I don't want to rub it in or anything but in bygone times your people made very strict laws against the use of the Irish language by the Irish people. Now I'm not saying that that is the sole reason for the language's disappearance from many places in Ireland but it did help to bring about a state of affairs which hastened the decay of the mother-tongue and that's why you get many ignorant Irishmen, like our friend here, who have no knowledge at all of their own country's language.'

That didn't please the Limerickman at all and when he got the opportunity he drew me aside and whispered:

'I don't think it's a very nice thing you did just now, siding with an Englishman against your own countryman.'

And that's the strangest thing about the situation. The Limerickman would be as loyal to his country and to his comrades as the next but he didn't seem to think that he was betraying anything by knocking the Irish language. He's like the young lad from Dublin that I heard saying in the digs last year when the jazz came over the wireless: 'Listen, boys, wouldn't it just remind you of Ireland?'

But, alas, that was the only Ireland he knew, Ireland of the juke-box, Ireland the imitator.

I went across for the Rosary after dinner tonight. A fairly good crowd comes along regularly. Many of the men in this town are excellent Catholics.

I suffered a lot down among a gang of Englishmen today for I had to go down to fill the place of a man that didn't turn up for work. There was no style to their talk and I was fed up to the back teeth by the time the first break came along. They're a queer crowd, I must say: chattering away like a gaggle of children or geese and saying nothing at all. If I thought I'd have to stay with them for the rest of the week, I wouldn't come in at all. And, do you mind, they think they are much more clever than the Irish and they thought anything I said was a great joke.

I'm living among these odd people for more than six years now and I don't take to them any better than I did the first day. It's not that I hate them like a number of Irishmen do; indeed, quite otherwise. But they make me tired with their strange ways and I love to get away from them all the time.

A couple of lads from Kilkenny are in the digs with me and we have great crack reminiscing about that town and the characters in and around it. Kilkenny people have one virtue that most from other counties don't have and that is—they have a great sense of fun. They're a quiet people too, and you seldom find them looking for rows. They are more knowledge-able about things than most others and I think the reason for this is that the Christian Brothers have very good schools there—and also they go to the pictures a lot. You can say what you like about the pictures but there's no doubt but that they teach a person plenty and give them some understanding about what goes on outside their own little town.

One or two of the lodgers are talking about going home at Easter, and isn't it well for them? It's a fashion that is growing up in England nowadays—people seizing the opportunity for the short Easter holiday at home.

Many of the young people like to spend three days or so in Dublin rather than hang around this place.

Without waiting to see if the absentee had come back or not, I went back to my own gang today because I couldn't stand working with the English crowd any longer. Poor Andrew is getting very tired of the work here and I can see that East Anglia is calling him. That's where these lads spend most of the year—in and around King's Lynn and Cambridge working for the farmers.

Most of the men down there are from Erris and Achill and they do well on piece-work with the farmers. Even today they live in small huts or 'bothies' and they feed themselves. Those who are any way careful can make a good bit of money while those who do not, have nothing to show for all their hardship beyond rheumatics and premature old age.

Today we started on the second line in the tunnel. The first line had been relaid by the night shift by the time we got along in the morning. The work was done with the help of a mobile crane—and the new line looked well with the clean ballast underneath it. If I can stand it until Easter, I don't much mind what happens after that. Things will be looking up by then and, as the old navvy said, there'll be smoke out of every chimney.

We spent the day shovelling old ballast into wagons—about forty of us all told and we had great 'gas' for a while. It's always like that when you get a large group in one place. The company gets lively and there is usually good chat and laughter all around. I suppose there's some reason for this if one could only make it out but all I can say is that I've always noticed it to be like that.

Shovelling is strange work. You feel it very heavy to begin with, but when you get over your first tiredness and have an energy or 'gimp' as they call it for work, you could keep on shovelling until Doomsday. I don't know if shovelling is any good for keeping you strong and healthy but I think it would probably do more damage than otherwise to a body in the latter end. At the same time, the old navvies who spent all their lives shovelling away are marvellously tough. You'd see old bucks that you'd have no great regard for with their bellies swollen from drinking pints, but well able to keep going with the shovel and pick in a way that would have a normal man exhausted.

I looked up at one stage and saw Andrew signalling to Charlie and myself to go over to where he was. When we reached him, he winked at us and drew us to one side.

'What's wrong with you now?' said Charlie, a little bit cross for he doesn't really like the conspiratorial manner Andrew adopts when he has some story to tell.

'What about the three of us walking out from here a while?' said Andrew, 'the gang here will be shovelling this stuff for the rest of the day and there are enough here to make sure that our absence won't be noticed.'

'By God, you're right,' answered Charlie, his annoyance evaporating.

'Let's skip it,' I said.

'Wait a minute,' said Andrew, 'we'll slink out one by one so that we won't be noticed at all.'

We had to give in to him so he went first and we followed him. We kept on walking until we reached the north entrance of the tunnel. On the way, we passed a couple of gangs but nobody paid any attention to us.

'I thought the oul' cow's days were over,' said Charlie as soon as we came out into the open.

'She's still being skinned,' Andrew replied.

Right enough the weather was pretty bad with the wind driving great black clouds across the sky and heavy enough showers falling every other minute. We nearly went back to work; but then we thought that, as we had come so far, we might as well stay out another little while. We came up through the cutting and into the wood and then, quite unexpectedly, saw a farmer's house just on the other side. We were just about to turn back when himself came out and saw us. He started to talk to us; and I was happy enough when he didn't attack us for being on his land without as much as by your leave.

Well, he chatted away, and fair play to the Erris lads, as soon as they saw an opportunity, didn't they ask him if he wanted any piece-work done. He started to scratch his head, just as they do at home in Ireland and, in the end, he said he did. He wanted to put in a drain but between the comings and the goings he hadn't got the chance of doing it so far. Andrew and Charlie began to bargain with him and soon had the whole thing fixed up. I stood there stupified, wondering how on earth we could serve two masters, the tunnel and the farmer. But I kept my mouth closed and it was arranged that the three of us would start on the drain on Monday morning. Two pounds ten shillings the chain (twenty-two yards) is what he agreed to give us.

As we made our way back to the tunnel, I queried the others about the business.

'Easy enough,' said Andrew, 'we'll come out on the company's bus on Monday morning the same as any other day but instead of going into the tunnel, we'll go working for the farmer. We'll earn two pounds ten a head and we'll be finished early where we'd be working longer hours for less pay down the tunnel.'

Then the thought struck him.

'What's stopping us drawing both pay-packets?' he asked.

'How do you mean?' I said.

'We'll shout in our numbers on Monday like we do any other day and then again in the afternoon. We can spend the day up with the farmer and no one will know that we're not somewhere along the tunnel.'

'Yes,' said Charlie, looking ahead as usual.

'But if we're found out, we'll have lost this job all for the sake of a couple of days with the farmer. We can get another month out of this, perhaps, and you won't get better than that around here these days.'

'Ah, you're too cautious,' said Andrew, 'we'll take a chance on it and if they sack us, let them go to hell.'

In the end we agreed though none of us mentioned that it was a crime and a sin to take money when we hadn't properly earned it. But what harm, the employers aren't behindhand in cheating their workers. Isn't the crowd we're working for here getting two pounds nine shillings a week for every man jack on the job and instead of paying it out to the men, as is intended, aren't they putting it in their pockets and giving us maybe ten shillings worth of sandwiches in the week?

When we got to the tunnel on Monday morning, along we went with the rest to the office where we called in our names and numbers. We jumped over the ditch then and made our way across the fields to the farmhouse. The pipes were ready in the yard; so we had to load them on the trailer and bring them down to the field. We took with us the 'grafts' to cut the trenches. These are like the loy but the blade is very narrow and the 'foot' short.

Andrew and Charlie laid out the work as they are knowledgeable in this kind of operation. We started digging as soon as we had decided the direction the trench would take. We only had to take out a graft's width of earth, eighteen inches

167

deep and lay the pipes reasonably even. We kept at it steadily and before we noticed it, each of us had the length of a chain done.

Down came the farmer's wife then with a huge jug of tea and a plateful of sweet cake. We were very grateful for this as it hadn't been mentioned when we made the bargain with the farmer but the poor woman had a generous instinct. It was still early in the day and we felt that we could finish the work before the evening fell. If we really put our minds to it. We were between two minds whether to finish it there and then or to get another day out of it. In the end, we thought it would be better to get it over and get back to the tunnel next day.

We all worked hard during the afternoon and, when himself came along about six o'clock to see how we were getting on, the job was almost finished. He walked around for a while inspecting the work but he couldn't find any fault with it. To tell the truth, the credit was all due to the other two for if I had been on my own, the job wouldn't have been at all well-done.

'I'll wager you,' said Andrew, 'that there'll be a great crop of wheat in this field when we come this way again.'

'Yes, if I have even a penny left to buy seed after I've paid the Irish,' joked the farmer.

He went off then and we finished the task. We brought the grafts up to the house and were paid our money. Twelve pounds he paid us and everybody was satisfied. And isn't it a great stack of money out of a person's pocket all in one day? But, of course, unless it was worth it, he wouldn't have coughed up. After that, it wasn't long until we got home after 'clocking out' at the office.

We sneaked into the tunnel next morning trying not to make ourselves too conspicuous in front of the foreman but there was no danger. We found out that all the gangs had been working together filling wagons and that no one could have said who was there and who wasn't. When Andrew heard this, his eyes lit up and a cunning look crossed his face and I guessed straight away what he had in mind.

'For God's sake, don't open your mouth,' I said, 'for I know what you're going to say—that we can work it again! But to hell with that. We succeeded this time but that's not to say that we can do it every day of the year.'

'True for you, Danny,' said Charlie, 'if we give in to him again, we'll be spending the summer in prison.'

'Bad luck to the two of you, you're no good,' said Andrew, disappointed that we couldn't spend another day with some farmer and draw our money from the tunnel crowd as well.

We saw a great bit of fighting at dinner-time today.

It happened that we were up near the first air-shaft when the whistle blew and we drifted over to the fire nearby waiting for the man with the tea to come. When he came by us, everybody started to crowd in on him—every man with his cup outstretched trying to be first to get his drop of tea. Some got spilt on one of the men in the jostling and he roared:

'It's easy knowing the Culchies never saw a queue. All they know is pushin' and shovin' and I'm all right, Jack, hump you.'

I don't rightly say if he was in earnest or not but, anyhow, the words were no sooner out of his mouth before another man answered him.

'I'm a Culchie,' he said, 'and I don't think any half-starved Jackeen* like you can teach me manners.'

'You're probably right about that,' said the first man—I wouldn't think he was a Dublinman even though the 'Culchie' called him a Jackeen—'When you weren't taught manners till now, I doubt you ever will.'

That's as much talk as there was. The Culchie grabbed the other man, the tea was spilt, and there was a right set-to. We formed a ring around them and they began to fight in earnest. I'd think they were as strong and as fast as each other but the Jackeen (if he was a Jackeen) was maybe a bit more intelligent. They stood there, anyway, in their shirts, pants and boots, lamming away at each other in anger and hate; and what matter but there was so little reason for the whole thing.

The Culchie got in a terrific blow on the point of the jaw and

* An equally contemptuous term for a native of Dublin.

you could have heard the noise down at the other air-shaft. The Jackeen was badly shaken but he didn't fall. It wasn't long after that till he got the Culchie with as fine a punch on the nose as you ever saw. The Culchie lost his reason after this and his two arms flailed away as he gnashed his teeth like a madman. The other man managed to avoid these attempted blows and he got in a couple of punches on Culchie's mouth. After that, Culchie started to collect his wits for he must have known that he'd get nowhere the way he was going. He avoided a punch from Jackeen and whipped in with another blow to the jaw. There must have been great power behind that one for it pole-axed Jackeen.

Culchie was panting away as he looked down at the man on the floor. I don't think he would have lasted if he hadn't floored the other man. Then, whatever devil got into him, he let a wild yell out of him and drew back his foot to kick the man that was down in the ribs. If he had succeeded in that, I don't know what state the other poor man would have been in but, thank God, Handlebars caught him by the elbow and pulled him to one side before he could put in the boot.

'Don't boot him, Pat,' said Handlebars. 'Play the game, man. You beat your man fair and square, what more do you want.'

The bucket of tea was gone and no more to be had so we had to put up with a dry dinner.

We went over to the church after supper. The Stations of the Cross was on and the Stabat Mater reminded me of home. To bed early.


Andrew and big Geordie had a sharp exchange this morning shovelling ballast out of two wagons. This is how it started. Our gang and Bill Donovan's gang were emptying ballast wagons side by side. When the ballast was all out, we took a bit of a rest while the wagons were taken out by the diesel; the men began to talk about the work they had done—how much one man had thrown out in so much time and so forth. This Geordie was boasting about how well the miners could handle a shovel compared with other people. He asserted that he had spent some time in the coal-mines and that the miners were better workers than the Paddies any day.

Andrew started calling him out, saying that he could shovel as well as any man that ever went down a mine even though he had spent most of his life working with farmers. The diesel was coming back by this time with a long line of wagons full of stones and the other lads said they should have a bet on it between them. When this was put to them, they couldn't draw back and they agreed to take a wagon each and see who would be first to have his wagon emptied.

The rest went into the other wagons, three to each one and Andrew and Geordie went into a wagon each. Indeed, the company made no profit while the two men worked like the devil as everyone was just standing around watching the pair. You could see the two piles of stones like a fistful of sand that you'd let go of, they were going so quickly.

Both of them got up on the piles of stones and prepared their places, shovelling away as if they had sweeping brushes in their hands. Andrew bared the floor of his wagon quicker than the other man and that was a great help to him. Once you have found the bottom of the wagon, you can push the shovel under the stuff easier than through the upper part. The foreman had a watch in his hand to time them but it could be seen that there was little to choose between them. The foreman would throw a glance at us now and again as much as to say we should get on with our jobs and our own shovelling but we were far too interested in the contest to pay much attention to him. Most of the attention was because here was an Irishman and an Englishman vying with each other with the honour of their respective countries depending on them. Each of the two men had good support and, although nothing was said, we felt that the Englishmen in the two gangs were hoping that Geordie would win.

Both men were perspiring heavily by now and the dust was rising thickly all around them. Neither of them raised their heads but kept on shovelling like two automatons. Charlie and I were praying to ourselves that Andrew wouldn't crack after saying that he could do as much as any miner; and we stood by the side of the wagon to see how he was making out. It was hard to say who had most stuff thrown out but it seemed to me that Geordie just had it over Andrew. I thought he was managing to get more up on his shovel. I don't think it was ever so quiet in the tunnel since work started there for hardly any noise was being made by anybody else.

Geordie was bathed in sweat by now—a fine strong stump of a man he was, all right—and I think he was a bit more tired than Andrew. 'It's easy to see,' I thought, 'the man who learned his trade on the bog—he has more stamina than is usual.' The floors of the two wagons were clear of stones by now and all that was left was a pile in each of the four corners. It was a half an hour since they had started and they hadn't had even one minute's rest, either of them.

They tackled the corners with vigour, Andrew tall and thin, Geordie, short and sturdy, throwing out the ballast like bullets from a gun. Andrew was out of his corner maybe a half minute before the other man and he went for the second corner like a madman. Geordie whipped around then and started on the other corner like a man shovelling golden guineas into a bag all for himself; but it was no good. Andrew got through what he had left like a knife and he leaped out of his wagon before Geordie had even started on his last corner.

Forty minutes it had taken him and Geordie was only a couple of minutes behind him. It was a great feat altogether and we were proud of Andrew. I think we were also happy that Geordie hadn't been too badly defeated for he had done a great bit of shovelling and he shook hands with Andrew when he climbed down off his wagon.

The three of us spent the afternoon drawing concrete in barrows and as the barrows have pneumatic tyres, it was nice light work, happily. Many covet this job during the laying of concrete.

Like the old lad long ago that was working behind the mixer, filling it up with sand and stones: this young lad came in on the job his first day and he was put hauling the stuff from the mixer in a barrow. The old lad didn't like a nice light job like that being given to the young fellow who had just come into the place and he started complaining to the foreman about it. He claimed that the young lad should have been set shovelling and that he himself should have been given the barrow.

'Get back to your shovelling,' roared the foreman, 'sure you know nothing about machinery.'

And that's all the satisfaction he gave the old chap!

It looks as if they'll be working here through Easter. If so, I'll not come in on Easter Sunday or Easter Monday and I don't care what they say or do to me. There are men here that wouldn't give up working at any time. If there were eight days in the week, they'd work every single day. Greed is not the only cause of this but a lack of imagination also in the workers. Most of them don't realize that there's fun and pleasure to be had in life—apart from being in a pub every evening. If they were back home, they'd probably have plenty of sport such as hurling or handball, or maybe throwing the weight down at the cross-roads. Here, there's nothing for them most of the time except drinking and gambling.

I remember a couple of years ago when McAlpine was building the reservoir down at Pitsford, some of the men would stay working until ten o'clock at night. Many of them were so keen on overtime that it was said that they had to be beaten out with a stick in the evenings. And you've people back home in Ireland saying that we're a lazy people and that if we were good workers, the country would prosper. If we are lazy, then it is a mental and not a physical laziness. I think myself that if wealthy people back home used their money to start industries suitable to their localities, the workers would keep their part of the bargain and everybody would be better off in the end.

Didn't I see myself two Englishmen that came into our part of the country—one of them to Barna and the other to Knock-nacarragh at the top of Salthill—and started a couple of under-takings. The man at Barna bought a piece of the old wood, cleaned it out and started to grow flowers of all kinds there. That man today has lorries carrying flowers for people all over the country who order them and a good many people in the district are employed by him. The other man went and started a little seaweed industry and is now giving employment to about sixty of the lads round the place. It's the same with the French-man over at Clifden—the lobster man I'm talking about. He saw that there was a good demand for lobsters and seized his opportunity. What's wrong with the moneyed people back home that they don't put their money working like that both for their own sakes and for the poor? Something is wrong; but it's not the poor man who has to come across to England to earn his living that is to blame—it's those who wrap themselves in luxury.

Poor Charlie was crippled again today with a pain in his stomach. He's had it for a long time now and, instead of trying to keep his spirits up, Andrew teases him, saying things like:

'That's a bad dose, Charlie. That'll kill you. By God, you'll have to have the knife. There's no damn good in those bottles you're always knocking back.'

'Blast you anyway for a thief,' the sick man would answer, 'wouldn't you have the kind word for me sometime? If you had this pain, you wouldn't be in all that form for joking.'

Charlie is always very thick with me because I pay some attention to his illness; and he'd spend hours telling you about the pains in his belly.

I had a whole week's pay to draw today. Seventeen pounds I got, after deduction of the insurance stamp. That wasn't too bad, even if the hours are long itself.

# 9

# An Exile's Homesickness

———◆◆◆———

*Good Friday*. I always feel very guilty on this day and I'm always glad when it's over. There's a great difference between Good Friday at home and Good Friday here.

To the English, it's only the beginning of the holiday, a day on which you eat hot-cross buns; and they work on that day so that they can have Easter Tuesday off. Some of the Irish are just as bad and they think nothing of going out drinking and celebrating that night. Well, it wasn't like that for the old people who would have nothing to eat but a bit of dry bread or to drink but a drop of black tea throughout the whole day and who would spend most of the time saying the Rosary.

First thing in the morning, I felt I wanted to get home. Some of the lads were talking of going to Dublin for Easter and I began to think of doing the same. Like Raftery* long ago, I had no peace until I gave in to my urge.

When I got home from work, I gave myself a good scrubbing, put on my Sunday suit, took three spare collars and a toothbrush, stuck a razor in my pocket and made my way to the station. I was as excited as a child as I thought of the trip particularly as I had started out quite spontaneously. I was amazed at how many were making their way home.

* An eighteenth century wandering Irish poet who wrote a well-known poem about his longing to be back in his own county.

As usual, I slept most of the way from Rugby onwards. I never can stay awake with the noise of the wheels and the swaying of the train on the rails. As we crossed Conway Bridge, the noise woke me up but I fell asleep again; and when I woke up again, I saw the sea stretched out like a mirror under the moonlight.

I got a great kick out of going through the Customs shed at Dun Laoire in the morning with nothing whatsoever to declare. I had a good breakfast in that café that is directly opposite Westland Row Station. You have to be impressed with the waitresses in the restaurants in Dublin—they're so chatty and contented in themselves unlike their counterparts in England.

When I finished, I moved off down town to have a look at the place. Isn't it maddening that I know more about London than I know about Ireland's first city?

For instance, I wouldn't know where in Dublin to look for the kind of company I frequent over there—that is, if there is any equivalent. Here in Dublin, there are Irish of all kinds—rich, poor, intelligent and ignorant—but in England, for the most part, there is only one kind of Irishman and that is the worker. If you live long enough over there, you begin to think that all the Irish are working-class—which, of course, is not true.

I bought an Easter Lily* on the Bridge and walked slowly up O'Connell Street. I bought a copy of *Inniu* and of *Aiseiri* in Eason's and took them in with me to the Tower Bar. I knocked back two pints very pleasantly while I listened to the chat all around me. The atmosphere in the pubs here is marvellous compared with those over the way. There's a depth and a vigour in the talk you hear; and the odd time you get women present, they're not screaming and roaring like the English women. In Dublin pubs, you'd know that the drink and the conversation were the most important things; but in England, the drink is only an excuse for playing cribbage and darts. May our lovely Irish pubs last forever!

The two things I noticed most here in Dublin were the prettiness of the women and the poverty of many of the people. If you had nothing else to remind you that you were in Ireland,

* Sold at Easter to commemorate the 1916 rising.

the women's faces would confirm the fact for you. Irish women facially, don't resemble the women of any other country, I think. High cheek-bones, freckles, grey-blue eyes and black curly hair are what you notice most about the women in this city. And it's amazing how many girls have those characteristics when you recall how much Danish and English blood has been here for so many centuries.

Alas, the other matter, the poverty is as noticeable here. You'd be hard put to count how many people passed you by in old, worn clothes. Most of them are in threadbare overcoats and their shoes are badly worn down. You don't see people like that in England at all nowadays; and, in themselves, they epitomise the bad way in which Ireland finds herself.

Two hours it took on the diesel to Kilkenny. On my way home from the station, I dropped into Stephen Brennan's for a drink. Stephen nearly had a fit when he saw me coming in.

'Oh, by God,' he cried, 'I thought you were gone!'

'Gone where?' I asked him.

'Over the way,' he said.

'Well, I've come back,' I answered.

'Well, by the honey, England must be a great country,' he marvelled as he pulled me a pint. They'll all be talking now about the great earnings in England that enable people to come home again after a bare seven weeks.

My father and mother got a right start when I walked in the door on them. The old lady started cooking straight away and the old man was tremendously bucked up.

Thank God, the weather is great and looks like continuing. It's nice to see the active young boys playing among themselves out on the grass—a sure sign that the country is not beaten yet. If things improve gradually and if everyone can earn a decent living, we'll have to have plenty of people to enjoy what comfort will be going!

I went to Confession in the Abbey; it was like Heaven inside there were so many candles burning and flowers decorating the altar. Ireland is the most Catholic country in the world; you can be sure of that.

*Easter Sunday.* A lovely morning, thanks be to God. To Mass early in the Black Abbey with my mother. The people are lovely and happy here together, greeting each other kindly coming from Mass. It's only an ignorant man that would say life is better over the way, despite the money you can earn.

I met my father after eleven o'clock Mass and we walked down town. A group of cyclists from Dublin came down Patrick Street and stopped for a rest on the Parade. They were happy, loud-voiced, amused by the country people but for all that full of harmless fun. There was a good crowd already there as we made our way into Larry's. Larry and the lads were amazed to see me coming back so soon.

I ate a fine Irish dinner: bacon, cabbage, roast and boiled potatoes with a nice sweet to follow. I was the only one of the family present. Kevin is in Daventry, Noel in Hampshire, Brian in Sussex and Dympna, our only sister, in London. It's the same story in many houses here and, indeed, all over Ireland.

I got out the bike after dinner and went out the Callan road to have a look at the countryside. Spring is in full sway here while it's only the beginning across the water. The little peaks of Tullaroan were on my right hand side, Mount Leinster and the other mountains on my left, all standing out clearly against the background of the sky and directly in front of me, the majestic mass of Sleivenamon, unchanged from the time of Finn Mac-Cool. Round these parts lived Humphrey O'Sullivan, the diarist. He left us an accurate and lively account of the lives of the people here and the doings of his time.

Humphrey always lamented the oppression of the Irish by the English; but in this lovely countryside, the Irish are in command now—those of them that are left. The Irish language has taken itself away from these rich lands—across the Corrib and into the bleak lands of Erris and the islands off the west coast. One man and his few cattle live here where, in O'Sullivan's time, twenty people lived—Irishmen speaking Irish. What could have been better—to give a good livelihood to the people when they were here so that they would have self-respect and treasure their national language, or to try to bring Irish back from the grave so that it can be on Irish lips again?

Gloomy thoughts, and this is Easter, the time of hope and courage; and all I have is two more days before I have to get back into that tunnel at Rugby. To hell with them for thoughts!

The old lady and myself spent a long time after I came in sitting together talking about life in general. More than anything else, she'd love me to remain at home but I can't.

I spent an hour down at the corner in front of the Savoy after tea. A crowd gathers there every Sunday night to discourse about the world and its ways or to talk about anyone who happens to be passing by. Great fun is had sometimes by one of the playboys imitating the neighbours in a harmless spirit of fun. But that's one of the nice things about the people here—they can see the good side of things always. They all know one another and take a rise out of each other at times.

Like some of the boys who try to sneak into the fourpenny part of the cinema so that those who are up in the one-and-sixpenny part won't know: they wait until the picture has started and then they slip into the cheap place, a handkerchief up to their faces so that they won't be recognized and their lapels turned up. The doorman lets them by and, when they think they're away with it, he roars at the top of his voice:

'Come along, now, gentlemen, no need to hide your features, we all know you. It's no disgrace to go in the fourpennies and I'm sure the fourpence is honestly come by.'

A great roar of joy goes up from the friends of those trying to sneak in; and all the unfortunates can do is to sit with their heads bent down hoping that the fun won't last too long.

I don't know if the same tricking goes on in other Irish towns. Not in Galway, anyhow; but it certainly adds to the fun anywhere.

I didn't bother taking a drink tonight. I walked home at my ease enjoying the healthy night air. I stood at the gate looking up at the stars. It's the same sky that will be over me when I get back to Northampton in a couple of days time—but I feel more natural with it here.

I'm really lucky so far as the weather is concerned anyhow. Today is altogether beautiful and I don't remember when I felt so well.

Myself and the old lad mooched off down town before eleven. People were walking around at their ease and the girls looked lovely in their summer dresses. The amount of lovely women that are in this town! Times I think it might be nice to settle down and marry one of them. For a man like myself that has reached the age of thirty, it's not at all too soon to be thinking of the like. Indeed, I suppose a lot of us would do it if we could stay at home but what's the good of talking about that? I've often said that it's a good thing to stay in the place in which you were born and where the seven generations before you lived. You'd feel you belonged to the place, that your roots were there, so to speak, instead of feeling like visitors as we do in England. If there was work to be had here, there's not a town in Ireland could compare with it, for they're a generous light-hearted people, the Cats.*

I went up Ormond road during the afternoon on the bike, keeping going for an hour or so until I came to the boreen that brings you out at St. Fiachra's Well on the bank of the Nore. They say there's a cure in that water and I remembered that day I went down there hoping that my sight would improve so that I could join the army. It wasn't long since we had come to Kilkenny from Galway and I was heart-broken after the old place. I thought the best way to get back there was to enlist in the First Battalion which was Irish-speaking—up at Renmore. I enlisted all right but not until long after I had been up at St. Fiachra's Well and by that time I was as much in love with Kilkenny as with Galway.

I walked along by the river shoving the bike in front of me until I came to Fennessey's Mill. The weir above the mill was murmuring away sleepily with the whiteness of the spray standing out against the dark waves of the stream. The fresh green leaves of the trees added to the beauty of the place and the old empty skeleton of the mill under its curtain of ivy stood for a way of life that is over for ever. The old wheel won't turn again and nothing will be ground there ever. But people will get pleasure from the sight of it for some time to come and that in itself is something.

Next summer people will come and walk along this way, parents and their children, a young Franciscan brother, boys imagining to themselves that they are wild red Indians, a

* For some reasons, Kilkenny people are known as 'Cats'.

courting couple hand in hand—and the perpetual fishermen. But Joe Soap will be over in the Midlands shovelling and digging away and nothing worth calling a river nearer than a hundred miles to him.

There was a nice crowd in Stephen's place tonight and the pint was magnificent. I met Sean Whelan, my old friend from Ballyfoyle there and we had a good bout of conversation. Paddy Dollart came in too, and we started talking about the time we were working on the railway in Warwickshire. Sonny Campbell came along then to bore us about his job with Wimpey in Stevenage and with his job with McAlpine in Chatham, and about the wealth you can amass from them— you'd think nothing of twenty pounds or anything under it!— but there's no danger that Sonny will move across as long as he can squeeze out the extra day for himself here.

Sometimes, I think he's an agent for some crowd that want to leave this country desolate altogether for he never gets tired of advising people to go across the water and not be wasting their lives here. He's like many others that are lucky enough to be able to stay at home; he likes to be praising the place over the way and running down his own. But what harm? As Sean says: 'You must listen to thunder.'

*Tuesday, 23.4.1957.* A bit cool today. My father and I spent a couple of hours in Larry's before dinner. There weren't many there; the holiday is over. I savoured the atmosphere of the place to the full: a peaceful quietude and the steady tick-tock of the old-fashioned clock above the bottles on the top shelf, the heavy-sweet smell of the porter and the low voices of the men talking quietly as if they did not wish to break the silence. Larry shook hands with me as I was leaving and wished me a good journey.

I found the time trying while I was hanging around waiting to leave the house. The old lady was very sad even though many's the time before I had gone away. Will anyone ever get used to parting?

Two hours on the train to Dublin. I had a good short holiday and I shouldn't be unhappy. But after all, I envy the cattle lying on the green grass of Ireland gazing cow-like at the

C.I.E.* carriages riding by. But even the cattle are trundled across too, like the Paddies and Brigids of Ireland.

Coming into Dun Laoire, I saw men in white clothes playing cricket and, somehow I felt annoyed. A young man and his girl were walking by themselves down below us in the golden evening sunlight. It's well for you, my friend, that every day you arise can be spent round about this place.

The White Boat† is laden down with people. Most of them, I fancy, like myself, returning after Easter. I can see, too, that others are going across for the first time. On my right, there is a little group from Connemara talking in Irish. If I live at all, surely that's Horse Flaherty down below! If it is, we'll have great sport in no time!

Doesn't Dun Laoire look beautiful with the mountains behind it? The quay is lined with little sailing boats, and wooden rowing boats. The wealthy own them, those who can stay behind here.

And then, without warning, she drifts from the quay. Wasn't I the inattentive one that I didn't see them getting ready? I can sense the old feeling in my stomach that I get each time I leave Irish soil, but it won't last long. I'm getting used to it now.

The Wicklow mountains are on the right, merging into the darkness of the night. Do their colours change, I wonder, like the Twelve Pins.‡ The sun has gone down now but there are faint golden rays in the west still. For a minute, I have a vision of Lough Corrib and again I get that sensation in my stomach.

Somewhere around me a man is singing the 'Rose of Tralee.' Someone else yarns.

We're a great people, surely.

* The National Transport System.
† The boat from Dun Laoire to Holyhead.
‡ A range of mountains in Co. Galway.